IMAGES
of Aviation

A CENTURY OF FLIGHT

Full circle: Brian Jones, of the UK, and Bertrand Piccard, of Switzerland, overcame the last great challenge of twentieth-century flight when they made the first circumnavigation of the world by a balloon in the combination hot air-helium Cameron R-650 *Breitling Orbiter 3*. Between 1 and 21 March 1999 they covered 25,361 miles from Château d'Oex, Switzerland, to land near Dâkhla in Egypt, recrossing meridian 9° 27′ west, their starting line, on 20 March. They also completed another full circle, as this type of balloon is known as a Rozier, after Pilâtre de Rozier who made the first free flight in any form of aircraft, a hot air balloon, 216 years earlier. (Photograph: Jean-François Luy)

IMAGES
of Aviation

A CENTURY
OF FLIGHT

Compiled by
John W.R. Taylor, OBE

Dedicated to
Sir Sydney Camm
My mentor 1941-1947 and friend
who opened the door to a lifetime
of adventure in aviation

TEMPUS

Acknowledgements

It is impossible to thank all the friends and colleagues who provided over more than half a century the photographs and information that appear in this book. Those whose never-failing kindness has helped to fill worrying gaps during the past six months include Maurice Allward, Simon Ashmore of London City Airport, Col. Pil. Pasquale Aveta of the Italian Air Force, Richard Bellamy of Mission Aviation Fellowship, Philip J. Birtles, Hermann Betscher of the Historical Flight Research Committee Gustav Weisskopf, Peter M. Bowers, Capt. E.M. Brown, J.M. Bruce, Cdr James G. Carlton USN of *Naval Aviation News*, Attilio Costaguta of ICAO, Colin Cruddas of Cobham plc, Philip Dunnington of Cameron Balloons, Nigel Eastaway of the Russian Aviation Research Trust, Candy Elsmore of MOTAT, W.R. Christopher Foyle of Air Foyle, Peter H.T. Green, Dan Hagedorn of the Smithsonian National Air and Space Museum, Harry Holmes, Mike Hooks, Sqn Ldr Peter Izard of the British Berlin Airlift Association, Paul Jackson, Derek N. James, Philip Jarrett, Jay Levine of NASA Dryden Flight Research Center, Alec McRitchie of Short Brothers plc, Kenneth Munson, William O'Dwyer, David W. Ostrowski of *Skyways*, Roger W. Peperell, Edmond Petit, Tom Poberezny of the EAA, Norman Polmar, Alex Hay Porteous, Jeffrey P. Rhodes of Lockheed Martin, Bruce Robertson, Jerry Shaw of the Fleet Air Arm Museum, Andrew Siddons of Rolls-Royce, Sergei I. Sikorsky, Kristin Snow of Air Tractor, John Stroud, Michael Stroud, Gordon Swanborough, James B. Taylor and Michael J.H. Taylor.

John W.R. Taylor
Surbiton
April 1999

Contents

A myth of ancient Greece tells how Daedalus built wings of feathers and wax to escape, with his son Icarus, from imprisonment by Minos, King of Crete. Exhilarated by the freedom of flight, Icarus flew so high that the sun melted the wax of his wings and he was killed.

After coming to the throne in 863 BC, Bladud, the legendary ninth King of Britain, is said to have become one of the countless men who attempted to fly with home-made wings. This portion of a genealogy prepared for King James I by Thomas Lyte in 1605 shows Bladud and the imaginary Temple of Apollo in the city of Trinovantum (London), on to which he fell 'his body being broken into many pieces'.

One

The Origins of Flight

No one should have been surprised when the age-old dream of powered, winged, flight became reality at the beginning of the twentieth century. A Greek myth telling how Daedalus made wings of feathers and wax to enable his son Icarus and himself to escape imprisonment by Minos, King of Crete, had been familiar for well over 2,000 years. England had its own legendary birdman in the person of Bladud, ninth King of Britain and discoverer of the healing waters of Bath, who was said to have met a similar end to that of Icarus, in a flying accident at the time of the Biblical prophet Elijah.

More significantly, the Chinese had been flying a primitive form of aircraft in the shape of kites for at least twenty-two centuries. The mediaeval traveller Marco Polo related how some were used to help mariners assess their prospects for a successful voyage. A man was sent aloft on a giant kite which, if it flew steadily, was regarded as a good omen. Unstable flight, especially if the unfortunate 'pilot' was killed, suggested that it would be unwise to set sail for a while.

The chance discovery of a small wooden model during archaeological excavations at Saqqara in Egypt, in 1898, pointed to a far more fascinating possibility. It was stored in a box at Cairo Museum for many years, among carved representations of birds dating from the time of the Pharaohs. But no bird has a flat straight wing with what would be regarded today as a high-lift aerofoil section, or a body with the rear portion of narrow elliptical shape and

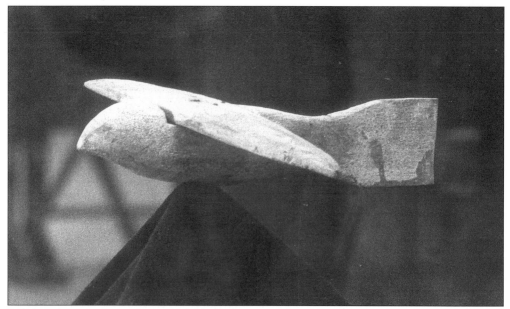

Exhibited near the treasures of Pharaoh Tutankhamun, in Cairo Museum, this small wooden model is the earliest known artefact displaying major features of an aircraft. Could a full-scale version have flown as a glider 300 years BC?

a deep vertical tail fin. Could the ancient Egyptians have experimented 2,300 years ago with a full-size version of this artefact that so clearly resembles a modern glider?

One and a half millennia after that model was carved, the English scientist-monk Roger Bacon wrote his *Secrets of Art and Nature*, dating from about 1250 and translated in 1659. He asserted: 'It is possible to make engines for flying, a man sitting in the midst thereof, by turning only about an instrument, which moves artificial wings made to beat the air, much after the fashion of a bird's flight'. He admitted that he had never seen the flying machine to which he referred, but was 'exceedingly acquainted with a very prudent man who hath invented the whole Artifice.' His reported UFO might have seemed more convincing two centuries later when the great Leonardo da Vinci, best remembered for his painting of the *Mona Lisa*, sketched but did not build such an apparatus, worked by the pilot's arms and legs.

The concept of flapping wings powered by a man's muscles should have been buried in 1680, when G.A. Borelli published his *De Motu Animalium* which set out to prove that human muscle-power could never be adequate to replicate bird-flight. Events took a more positive turn when it dawned on a few individuals that, as smoke (or hot air) rose above a fire, it might be possible to harness this 'gas' to lift a balloon. It was accepted until the second half of the twentieth century that the hot-air balloon was invented by the French brothers Joseph and Étienne Montgolfier. Research by historians in Portugal then produced conclusive proof that the true pioneer was a Brazilian-born priest named Bartolomeu de Gusmão. According to a manuscript written by Salvador Ferreira, Gusmão demonstrated a model hot-air balloon before King John V of Portugal, Queen Maria Anna, the Papal Nuncio (later Pope Innocent III) and others in the ambassadors' drawing room of the Casa da India on 8 August 1709. A painting of the event in the Museum of the City of São Paulo, Brazil, based on Ferreira's account, depicts a balloon of thick paper inflated by hot air from material burning in an earthen bowl inside a waxed-wood tray.

Another eighteenth century document, written by Father Lucas de S. Joaquim Pinheiro, reports that Gusmão subsequently tested a version of his invention large enough to carry a man. He states that 'this machine was sent up from the Place of Arms of St George's Castle and, having travelled one kilometre, fell down on the turret in the western part of the Place which was at that time the Terreiro do Paço.'

Recording such apparent evidence detracts nothing from the Montgolfiers, who perfected the practical hot-air balloon seventy-four years after Gusmão's model flights. It was in a *Montgolfière*, on 15 October 1783, that Jean-François Pilâtre de Rozier became the first human recognised officially to have left the ground in an aerial vehicle. Watched by a huge crowd, he ascended to a height of 85ft, where he remained, tethered by ropes, for four minutes and twenty-four seconds. On 21 November, this same volunteer aeronaut completed the first free flight of around $5\frac{1}{2}$ miles across Paris in another *Montgolfière*, accompanied by the Marquis d'Arlandes.

Little more than a week later, on 1 December 1783, Professor J.A.C. Charles made a two-hour flight, with Marie-Noel Robert, in a balloon inflated with 'inflammable air', which we now know as hydrogen. The two basic types of balloon that have continued with little change to this day had been produced. In 1794 the balloon made its military debut as a reconnaissance vehicle, able to observe enemy movements 'over the hill', at the battle of Fleurus in Belgium. Through the nineteenth century the hydrogen balloon was developed gradually into the powered, navigable airship which could be flown in any direction, regardless of the wind that dictated the flight path of balloons. But the future of flying still rested with those who dreamed of soaring on wings, like the birds.

The man whose work gave heavier-than-air flight the kick-start that it needed, earning him universal acceptance as 'the Father of Aerial Navigation', was Sir George Cayley of Brompton Hall, Yorkshire. He was first to state that a means of obtaining lift (wings) had to be separate from a method of providing thrust (propulsion). He recognised that the

8 August 1709. The first demonstration of a model hot-air balloon, built by Bartolomeu de Gusmão, is depicted in this painting by Bernardino de Sousa Pereira displayed in the Museum of the City of São Paulo, Brazil. A version large enough to carry a man is said to have been tested later.

21 November 1783. Start of a 5½ mile flight across Paris by Pilâtre de Rozier and the Marquis d'Arlandes in a *Montgolfière* hot-air balloon. This first aerial journey in history was not relaxing for the Marquis, who was commanded by de Rozier to maintain height by stoking the on-board fire repeatedly with fresh straw. When the fire burned holes in the fabric, and caused some of the structural ropes to break, he had to act as a fireman with a wet mop.

essentials for a successful heavier-than-air vehicle were stability, to ensure steady straight and level forward flight, an efficient control system and some kind of power plant. This last requirement would not be met until long after his death in 1857.

Cayley's earliest successful design, in 1804, took as its basis one of the most ancient airborne devices. A kite-like wing was propped up at 6° at the front of a 5ft-long rod. The rear part of the rod was attached by a universal joint, enabling cruciform tail surfaces to be moved up and down, and from side to side, to control the direction of flight. The result was the simplest form of what was to become the conventional configuration of an aeroplane throughout most of the twentieth century.

The most productive phase of Cayley's experiments did not begin until he was in his seventies. He had realized for a long time that a cambered wing would produce more lift than a flat surface and began designing full-size gliders with sail-type wings that became curved when the airflow filled them out. In a machine with triplane sail-wings and pilot-operated tail surfaces, he floated a ten-year-old boy safely downhill in 1849. Four years later his somewhat similar monoplane glider carried Cayley's reluctant coachman across a small valley behind Brompton Hall. Like the boy-carrier, it was provided with flappers that the pilot was intended to 'row' for propulsion. This shows that not all of Cayley's ideas were sound. But another English pioneer of the time very nearly got everything right.

London's Science Museum houses the original 20ft-span model of what its designer, William Henson, described as an Aerial Steam Carriage. It is a high-wing monoplane with all its component parts in the right places. When, in 1847, it was launched from an inclined ramp at Chard its small steam engine, driving two propellers, provided insufficient power for sustained flight. Imaginative drawings of a full-size Steam Carriage in flight over London and the Pyramids of Egypt were ridiculed, even in Parliament. It mattered little that the illustrations had been distributed by speculators more interested in attracting financial sponsorship than in serious engineering. Discouraged, Henson abandoned the whole project.

Today, the Aerial Steam Carriage is remembered as the first design for a complete powered aeroplane. Others followed during the second half of the nineteenth century. In France, a monoplane with a hot-air engine built by Félix Du Temple made a brief hop carrying a young sailor, after a downhill run at Brest in 1874. Ten years later in Russia, a hop of between 65 and 100ft was achieved by a pilot named Golubev in a large steam-powered aircraft designed by Alexander Fedorovich Mozhaisky, after similar assisted take-off.

French historians still claim that the honour of making the first recognised flight in a powered aeroplane belongs to their countryman Clément Ader. In his weird bat-wing *Eole*, with a 20hp steam engine, he is said to have travelled some 165ft through the air, eight inches above the ground, at Armainvilliers on 9 October 1890. It was not a controlled flight, and no one would pretend that the *Eole* offered promise of any future usefulness. The same was true of the immense steam-powered biplane tested by Sir Hiram Maxim at Baldwyn's Park in Kent. It certainly lifted itself briefly clear of its launch rails in 1894 before a guard-rail brought it to a halt; but Maxim was wise to end his experiments at that stage.

It was in this decade that one of the most respected of all flying's great pioneers came on the scene. Otto Lilienthal, in Germany, had written a book with the English title *Bird*

This model, in the Qantas Airways historical collection, represents one of the man-powered designs of the fifteenth-century Italian artist-inventor Leonardo da Vinci. Wings, of which only the spars are shown, were intended to be flapped by movement of the pilot's arms and legs, a completely impractical means of propulsion.

1849. The Qantas model of Sir George Cayley's glider, recognised as the first winged vehicle to lift a human being off the ground. A ten-year-old boy was floated a few yards downhill in Yorkshire, England. The 'three tiers of sail' contained 338sq ft of cloth; the wing span was 10ft, length about 20ft, height 10ft and weight without occupant about 130lb. Because of his success with this and his 1853 man-carrier, Cayley is regarded internationally as the true inventor of the modern aeroplane as well as founder of the science of aerodynamics.

1842. Shown over London in this imaginative drawing, William Samuel Henson's Aerial Steam Carriage was the first design in history for what we would now regard as a complete fixed-wing propeller-driven aeroplane of modern configuration. Owing much to the research of Cayley, it had double-surfaced cambered wings with spars and ribs, sixty-six years before such structures became standard practice. A 20ft-span model had insufficient power to fly but can still be seen in London's Science Museum.

Flight as the Basis of Aviation dated 1889. Not all of his conclusions were accurate, but, between 1891 and 1896, he built a succession of hang gliders in which he made around 2,500 successful flights of up to 985ft, many from an artificial hill near Berlin that is preserved as his memorial. He planned to instal a carbonic acid gas engine in one of them, to produce a powered aeroplane, but died on 10 August 1896, the day after one of his gliders suffered a structural failure and crashed in the Rhinower Hills, near Stöllen.

As the twentieth century dawned, the pace of progress quickened. An Australian named Lawrence Hargrave perfected the cellular box-kite that was to form the wing and tail configuration for many practical first-generation aeroplanes. In Germany, Otto and Daimler petrol engines promised the lightweight power plants for which aviation pioneers had yearned. The person who seemed most capable of putting together all the elements of progress was an eminent astronomer, Samuel Pierpont Langley, at America's Smithsonian Institution.

By 1895-1896 his No.5 and No.6 model aircraft, known as *Aerodromes*, were making flights of up to 4,200ft after launch by catapult from a houseboat on the Potomac River. Constructed of metal, with tandem wings spanning 14ft, each was powered by a steam engine driving twin propellers amidships. Langley received government funding to build a full-size version for potential military use. As a first step, in 1901, he completed a quarter-scale model which became the first aeroplane to fly with a petrol engine. On 7 October 1903 the 48ft span *Aerodrome* was ready for its first launch from a houseboat. It was

1874. French naval officer Félix Du Temple began in 1857-1858 with a clockwork-powered model monoplane that became the first aeroplane to take off under its own power, sustain itself in flight and land safely. This Qantas model shows the first full-size powered aeroplane ever built, again by Du Temple. It achieved its place in history by becoming the first to leave the ground with a pilot on board, but only after gaining speed down a ramp. Sustained manned flight awaited availability of an internal combustion engine.

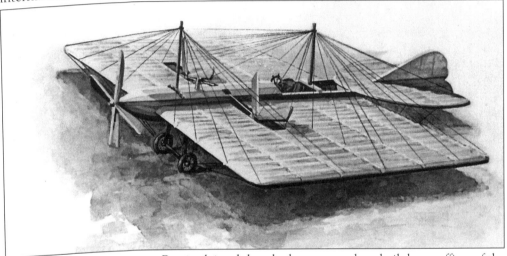

20 July 1882. For many years Russia claimed that the large monoplane built by an officer of the former Czarist Fleet, named Alexander Fedorovich Mozhaisky, flew twenty-one years before the Wright brothers' *Flyer*. Its two British-built Ahrbecker compound (petrol-steam) engines kept it briefly airborne after take-off down a ramp.

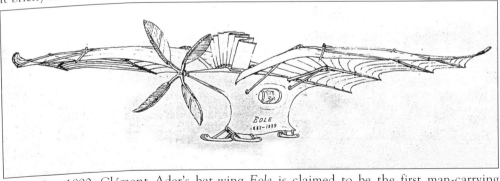

9 October 1890. Clément Ader's bat-wing *Eole* is claimed to be the first man-carrying aeroplane to lift itself from the ground for a brief first flight. It was, however, in no sense a practical design.

13

31 July 1894. Sir Hiram Maxim's giant biplane, powered by two 180hp steam engines, at the end of its brief flight which had been restricted to a height of two feet by guard rails. It spanned 104ft and weighed $3\frac{1}{2}$ tons when carrying a three-man crew.

1891. Otto Lilienthal became one of the greatest pioneers in the history of flying when he began testing this first of a series of fixed-wing hang gliders from a hill at Derwitz in Germany. Made of peeled willow wands, covered with waxed cotton cloth, they were controlled in flight by movement of the pilot's lower body to change the centre of gravity.

1893. Lilienthal built a wooden hangar on a hill known as the Maihöhe, near Steglitz. By taking off from its roof, 33ft above ground level, he made regular flights of up to 165ft. In 1895, he began sketching ideas for improved control by wing warping and moving surfaces, and planned to fit a carbonic acid gas engine to one of his latest aircraft. He sold examples of his hang gliders to other would-be flyers and although he was killed in 1896 his writings and flying provided the inspiration to men like Octave Chanute in the USA that sparked the ultimate success of the Wright brothers.

powered by a remarkable 52hp five-cylinder radial petrol engine designed by C.M. Manly, who also volunteered as pilot. Sadly, the aircraft fouled its launching mechanism and plunged into the Potomac. A second test, on 8 December, met a similar end. Although Manly was again unhurt, it marked the end of Langley's aviation research.

Claims of more successful early flights have caused heated controversy to this day. In Germany, an elderly civil servant named Carl Jatho achieved what he termed a *flugsprung* (flying leap) of 59ft in a triplane with an engine running on acetylene gas on 18 August 1903. Using components of this aircraft, and the same engine, he built a monoplane in which he made several flights of up to 196ft, at a height of around 11ft, in the autumn of that year. However, he did not have an engine powerful enough for true flight, in a very different aircraft, until 1909.

Aviation historians in New Zealand still suggest that a young farmer named Richard Pearse flew a small monoplane with a home-made engine at Waitohi on a date given usually as 31 March 1903. The claims are based on the evidence of local residents, many years later, who described how they had witnessed the event. Today, visitors to Auckland's Museum of Transport Technology and Social History can only marvel that the replica of Pearse's first aeroplane on display was designed by a man so remote from the aviation research being conducted, with little publicity or success, thousands of miles from New Zealand.

A contemporary of Pearse, and equally the subject of fierce controversy, was German-born Gustav Weisskopf, known in America as Gustave Whitehead. His supporters claim that he flew his Airplane No.21, with acetylene 'steam-type' power, for half a mile at a height of up to 50ft at Fairfield, near Bridgeport, Connecticut, on 14 August 1901. A drawing of the aircraft in the air appeared four days later in the *Bridgeport Sunday Herald*, illustrating a report by its sports editor who wrote that he had witnessed the flight.

7 October 1903. Langley's full-size *Aerodrome*, piloted by Charles Manly, plunges into the Potomac river after fouling the structure of its houseboat launcher.

31 March 1903. This replica of the aircraft built by Richard Pearse is a prized exhibit in the Museum of Transport Technology and Social History at Auckland, New Zealand. His reported 1903 flight will probably never be authenticated, but the genius of this young farmer, with no formal mechanical training, cannot be disputed.

14 August 1901. Gustave Whitehead, with his daughter Rose, in front of his Airplane No.21. Like Pearse, he has received scant credit for his efforts to fly at the beginning of the century.

Autumn 1903. On this monoplane, with superimposed elevator, Carl Jatho made flights of up to 196ft. Despite financial problems, by 1911 he had progressed to the first successful aircraft of steel-tube basic construction. Powered by a 50hp Argus engine, he flew it for more than a mile at a height of 85ft. In 1912, with a 100hp engine, he circled his home town of Hannover for eighteen minutes at around 3,000ft. He founded the Hannoversche Flugzeugwerke to produce what he called his *Stahltaube* (Steel Dove). Although outstanding, it was rejected by the German Army Command at the outbreak of the First World War in favour of products from more established manufacturers such as Fokker.

A photograph of the aircraft in the air, mentioned in the issue of *Scientific American* dated 27 January 1906, has since gone missing. A replica of Airplane No.21, as true as possible to the original and with an engine of equivalent power, made twenty flights of up to 330ft at Stratford, Connecticut, in December 1986. Another flew in Germany in 1997.

With all the benefits of nearly 100 years of hindsight, it is clear that the aircraft designed by men like Maxim, Ader and Whitehead offered little scope for development into vehicles of practical use. By comparison, a book entitled *Progress in Flying Machines*, written in 1894 by an engineer and glider builder named Octave Chanute, analysed all that had been attempted up to the time of Lilienthal and began a process that led to great things in the first decade of the twentieth century. The book inspired the brothers Orville and Wilbur Wright to embark on four years of patient aviation research, aided by a home-made wind tunnel. After testing a succession of thoroughly practical gliders, Orville made the first tentative hop of 120ft on their powered biplane *Flyer*, with a 12hp four-cylinder petrol engine of their own construction, near Kitty Hawk, North Carolina, on 17 December 1903. There is a photograph of that important moment in history. By the end of the day, Wilbur kept the *Flyer* airborne for fifty-nine seconds, covering 852ft on its fourth and last flight. During the five years that followed, the Wrights not only flew better than anyone else, but inspired others to build more capable aeroplanes.

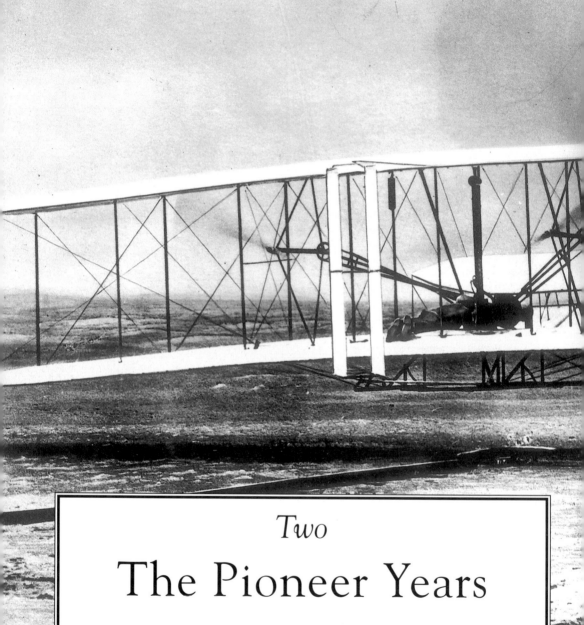

Two

The Pioneer Years

Brazilian-born Alberto Santos-Dumont made what is accepted as the first flight in Europe at Bagatelle, France, on 23 October 1906. He covered 197ft in his 14-bis tail-first box-kite biplane. On 12 November, he flew 722ft at 25.65mph. In 1905, Wilbur Wright had flown more than twenty-four miles in thirty-eight minutes during tests of the improved *Flyer III*. However, this was little known, and Santos-Dumont's distance and speed of November 1906 became the first official world records listed by the Fédération Aéronautique Internationale, formed on 14 October 1905.

The first attempt to produce a low-priced lightplane that could be built and flown safely by any would-be pilot was Santos-Dumont's *Demoiselle* (dragonfly) built in 1907. It flew only three times, but was revived in improved form, as shown, in 1909. Known as design No.20, it usually had a 35hp engine and span of 16ft 8¾in. Seated beneath the wings, the pilot had a stick to work the combined rudder-elevator and harness through which to control the warping wingtips through body movement.

Previous page: 17 December 1903. Orville Wright lifted the *Flyer* off its launch rail at Kill Devil sandhills near Kitty Hawk at 10.35 a.m. for an undulating twelve-second flight. This historic first flight by a powered and controllable man-carrying aircraft, landing at a point as high as that from which it started, was witnessed by five local persons. One of them took this photograph which shows Wilbur running by the wingtip. After three more, longer flights that day, the aircraft was wrecked by a gust of wind. The aerospace adventure it had started, in a total flying life of ninety-seven seconds, would lead to other Americans walking on the Moon long before the century ended.

Every slat of the 'Venetian blinds' fitted to Horatio Phillips' series of bizarre experimental aircraft from 1893 was a narrow-chord wing. His flight of about 500ft on one of them, with four frames in tandem and a 22hp engine, in 1907, is now regarded as the first by a man-carrying aeroplane in the UK.

On 13 November 1907, Paul Cornu's twin-rotor helicopter, with a 24hp Antoinette engine, became the first rotating-wing aircraft to fly freely carrying a pilot, near Lisieux in France. Practical helicopters would not be built, despite worldwide interest, until the 1930s.

13 January 1908. Henry Farman's circular flight of more than one kilometre in an Antoinette-powered Voisin biplane marked the start of practical flying in Europe and earned him a 50,000-franc Deutsch-Archdeacon prize. On 30 October 1908 he made the first true cross-country flight in an aeroplane, from Bouy to Reims, a distance of $16\frac{3}{4}$ miles, in another Voisin.

England's greatest pioneer of the early 1900s was A.V. Roe. Having won a £75 prize awarded by the *Daily Mail* newspaper at a model-flying contest in March 1907, he built a full-size version of his model, with a 24hp Antoinette engine, at Brooklands motor racing track in Surrey. When a Royal Aero Club committee met many years later to decide who, officially, was the first British aviator to fly in the UK, it refused to regard Roe's flights in this aircraft, from 8 June 1908, as more than hops.

The Wright brothers made no flights between 16 October 1905 and 6 May 1908. On 14 May, they made the first two flights with a passenger, each carrying Charles Furnas, in their modified *Flyer III*. Pilot and passenger now sat upright, instead of lying on the wing. Since 1904, the Wrights had used the falling weight catapult in the foreground of this picture to assist their wheel-less biplanes into the air.

In 1908 Wilbur brought a new Wright Model A biplane to Europe. His 104 flights at Camp d'Auvours near Le Mans in France, totalling some $25\frac{1}{2}$ hours and carrying sixty passengers, gave fresh impetus to European flying. Another Model A, shown here, became the first aeroplane delivered for military use when Orville took it to the US Army base at Fort Myer, Virginia. A propeller failure caused it to crash during his tenth demonstration flight, on 17 September 1908. His passenger, Lt T.E. Selfridge, was killed. He was the first person to die in a powered aeroplane. The aircraft was rebuilt, and was followed by nine much improved Wright Models B and C, used by the Army for training.

S.F. Cody, a colourful American-born pioneer, built this British Army Aeroplane No.1 in HM Balloon Factory at Farnborough. On 16 October 1908, when it was powered by a 50hp Antoinette engine, he flew it 1,390ft at a height of 50-60ft over the adjacent Laffan's Plain. This was the first officially recognised flight by a practical powered aeroplane in Britain. Born Samuel Franklin Cowdery, Cody had taken the surname of Colonel W.F. 'Buffalo Bill' Cody when he toured the US and Europe with his own Wild West show. He began his aviation career with man-lifting multiple kite systems, which evolved into his powered aircraft. Built of bamboo, it was so impressive that a later version was nicknamed 'the Cathedral'.

J.W. Dunne was a talented fellow designer of Cody's at Farnborough, who believed that the best way of achieving stability in flight was with a V-wing tail-less configuration. One of his most successful aircraft was this 1909 biplane which could be left to fly itself while he sat back in the cockpit and wrote his test flying notes.

13 July 1909. A.V. Roe became the first British subject to fly an all-British aeroplane when he flew 100ft in this small triplane at Lea Marshes, Essex. With little money, he covered it with brown oiled paper and fitted a J.A.P. engine of only 9hp. On 23 July he flew it 900ft.

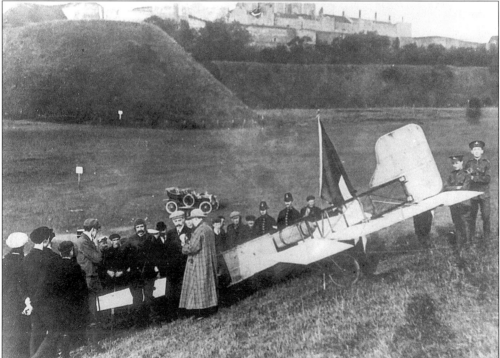

As one of a series of prizes intended to encourage aviation progress, the *Daily Mail* offered £1,000 to the first pilot who flew between England and France. The prize was won by Frenchman Louis Blériot on his Type XI monoplane, with a 24hp Anzani engine, on 25 July 1909. He is shown here by the aircraft after crash-landing in a meadow near Dover Castle. The flight from Calais had taken thirty-seven minutes. It was by far the most significant yet made, being the first between two countries over water. Britain seemed no longer an island protected from continental enemies by a stretch of sea.

GRANDE SEMAINE D'AVIATION DE CHAMPAGNE (Première Journée)
L'américain Curtiss et son biplan

Glenn Curtiss was the first American to fly after the Wrights, on his *June Bug* biplane, on 20 June 1908. He is shown here beside the propeller of his improved *Golden Flier* on which he won the Gordon Bennett International Trophy for the highest speed over a 20km course (47mph) at the world's first great aviation meeting, near Reims, in August 1909.

The first British flying meetings were held at Blackpool and Doncaster in October 1909. A Voisin biplane and three Blériot monoplanes are visible in front of the sheds at Doncaster. The most sensational flight was at Blackpool, where Hubert Latham in an Antoinette monoplane made the first-ever bad weather flight, in a gale, to avoid disappointing the crowd.

This strange-looking vehicle, built and piloted by Henri Fabre, was the first to make a powered flight from water, on 28 March 1910 at Martigues, in France. It was powered by one of Laurent and Louis Seguin's remarkable new 50hp Gnome rotary engines, with seven cylinders that rotated with the propeller around a stationary crankshaft, and it had a speed of 55mph. Today it is a prized exhibit at the Musée de l'Air in Paris.

27-28 April 1910. Louis Paulhan of France won one of the most exciting races in early aviation history by making the first flight from London to Manchester for a *Daily Mail* prize of £10,000. While he night-stopped at Lichfield, Claude Grahame-White made one of the first-ever short night flights in an effort to overtake him but had to land with engine trouble. Both pilots flew Farman biplanes with Gnome engines.

The first aircraft of any kind used on commercial passenger-carrying airline services was the Zeppelin LZ.7 *Deutschland* of Delag (Deutsche Luftschiffahrts Aktiengesellschaft). It carried a total of 142 passengers in seven flights between Dusseldorf, Frankfurt and Baden-Baden before being wrecked in a storm on 28 June 1910. Other Zeppelins resumed the operation and Delag flew a total of 107,211 miles, carrying 33,722 passengers in complete safety, from 1910 until the outbreak of war in 1914. LZ.7 was 485ft 6in long, had three 125hp Daimler engines and cruised at 33mph.

Pioneers like the Wrights believed that aeroplanes would be useful for military reconnaissance. The first hint of more aggressive roles was given on 20 August 1910, when Lt J.E. Fickel fired a rifle from this Curtiss biplane piloted by Charles F. Willard towards a target at Sheepshead Bay, New York. A Lewis machine-gun was fired by Capt. Charles de F. Chandler from a Wright Model B flown by Lt Thomas de Witt Milling on 2 June 1912.

23 September 1910. The Peruvian Georges Chavez took off from Brig in Switzerland, in a Blériot monoplane, to make the first flight over the Alps, via the Simplon Pass. He crashed from a height of 40ft on arrival at Domodossola, Italy, forty-five minutes later, and was fatally injured.

The company founded by the brothers Eustace, Horace and Oswald Short, now based in Belfast, received a contract from Wilbur Wright to build six Wright biplanes in March 1909, making it the first manufacturer of aeroplanes in the world. This Short No.2, built simultaneously for J.T.C. Moore-Brabazon (later Lord Brabazon of Tara) differed in many important details and had a 50-60hp Green engine. He used it on 30 October 1909 to win a *Daily Mail* prize of £1,000 for the first flight of one mile around a closed circuit by an all-British combination of pilot, aircraft and engine. Moore-Brabazon's flying had begun on a Voisin biplane in France in 1908, and he was awarded the Royal Aero Club of Great Britain's Aviator Certificate No.1 on 8 March 1910.

7 November 1910. The first freight carried by air comprised 542 yards of silk transported from Dayton to Columbus, Ohio, by Max Morehouse on a Wright Model B piloted by Philip O. Parmalee. The stunt cost the Morehouse-Martens Company $5,000, but it made a profit of more than $1,000, partly by cutting some of the silk into small pieces and selling them as souvenirs mounted on postcards.

The aircraft carrier of the future was pioneered on 14 November 1910 when Eugene B. Ely, one of Glenn Curtiss's exhibition pilots, flew a Curtiss-Hudson biplane off an 83ft runway erected over the bows of the scout cruiser USS *Birmingham* in Hampton Roads, Virginia. Its wheels dipped into the water before Ely could gain flying speed and head for land, $2\frac{1}{2}$ miles away. On 18 January 1911, he also made the first ship landing on a platform built over the stern of the armoured cruiser USS *Pennsylvania*. His aircraft was brought to a halt by hooks which caught ropes stretched across the platform between sandbags.

7 January 1911. Philip Parmalee again made history when he carried Lt Myron S. Crissy, who dropped the first live bomb from an aircraft, a Wright biplane, at San Francisco, California.

To establish the speed of his Antoinette monoplane, Hubert Latham arranged for Gordon Watney to drive level with him as he flew above the Railway Straight at Brooklands race track. The 60hp Mercedes had to sprint to catch the aircraft and then slow down to its speed of about 60mph with a 15mph back wind.

This is one of 100,000 letters and cards carried on the first British air mail service organised by Capt. W.G. Windham to mark the coronation of King George V. It was operated by pilots from Hendon's Blériot and Grahame-White flying schools between Hendon and Windsor between 9 and 26 September 1911. Earlier, Windham had shared a four-day operation in India with Henri Pequet, who made the first-ever official air mail flight on a Humber biplane, across the Jumna River from Allahabad, on 18 February 1911. Earl Ovington became US Air Mail Pilot No.1 when he carried a bag of mail six miles from Nassau Boulevard, New York, to Mineola, Long Island, in a Blériot-type Queen monoplane on 23 September 1911.

When Turkey objected to Italian military occupation of Tripolitania and Cirenaica, Italy declared war on 29 September 1911 and dispatched units with seventeen assorted aircraft to North Africa as part of its Expeditionary Force. An aeroplane was used in war for the first time on 22 October, when Capt. Piazza made a one-hour reconnaissance in a Blériot XI to observe Turkish troop positions between Tripoli and Azizia. The first bombs dropped in war were $4\frac{1}{2}$ lb Cipellis, from an Etrich Taube monoplane flown by Lt Gavotti on 1 November. On 10 January 1912 Piazza made the first air-drop of propaganda leaflets, inviting Arabs to desert the Turks. On 24 and 25 February he took the first wartime aerial reconnaissance photographs over Suani-Beni Adem, near Zanzur.

1 May 1912. Wilfred Parke was first to fly in an aeroplane with a fully enclosed cabin when he began tests of the Avro Type F at Brooklands. The trapdoor for entry was in the roof, and the pilot could poke his head through large circular holes on each side of the cabin for improved visibility in poor weather. A 35hp Viale engine gave the aircraft a speed of 65mph. Only one was built.

By 1912 many thousands of people flocked to Hendon aerodrome each summer weekend to watch the flying. The 45,000 who paid for admission, and many more outside, saw this Burgess-Wright piloted by F.P. Raynham win the Shell speed handicap race before the main event, the first Aerial Derby, won by Gustav Hamel on a Blériot in June.

When the Royal Flying Corps came into existence, with Military and Naval Wings, on 13 April 1912, it was decreed that the Aircraft Factory at Farnborough was to be retained as sole source of supply for its aircraft. This was disregarded by the Navy, which continued to buy aircraft from private companies like Shorts for what was soon renamed the Royal Naval Air Service. Londoners had their first sight of a seaplane when Frank McClean took off from Harty Ferry in the Short S.33 on 10 August 1912, flew through Tower Bridge, and skimmed under all the other bridges before alighting between Charing Cross and Westminster bridges.

The pioneer of really large aeroplanes for both transport and military use was Igor Ivanovich Sikorsky, chief engineer at the Russian Baltic Railcar Factory's aircraft division at St Petersburg. His S-21 *Bolshoi Baltiskiy* (Great Baltic), known usually as *Le Grand* (the Great One), was the world's first four-engined aeroplane when he flew it on 13 May 1913. It spanned 88ft, weighed 9,250lb and was powered by four 100hp Argus engines. On 2 August, it carried eight people for nearly two hours in its enclosed cabin.

20 April 1914. The capability of the young company formed by the famous sporting pilot Thomas Sopwith was demonstrated when Howard Pixton won the second contest for the Jacques Schneider seaplane trophy at Monaco in a Sopwith Tabloid. He also set a world speed record for seaplanes of 86.6mph over a measured 300km course.

St. Petersburg-Tampa
AIRBOAT LINE

Fast Passenger and Express Service

SCHEDULE:

Lv. St. Petersburg 10:00 A. M.
Arrive Tampa   10:30 A. M.

Leave Tampa   11:00 A. M.
Ar. St. Petersburg 11:30 A. M.

Lv. St. Petersburg 2:00 P. M.
Arrive Tampa   2:30 P. M.

Leave Tampa   3:00 P. M.
Ar. St. Petersburg 3:30 P. M.

Special Flight Trips

Can be arranged through any of our agents or by communicating directly with the St. Petersburg Hangar. Trips covering any distance over all-water routes and from the waters' surface to several thousand feet high AT PASSENGERS' REQUEST.

A minimum charge of $15 per Special Flight.

Rates: $5.00 Per Trip.   **Round Trip $10.**   **Booking for Passage in Advance.**

NOTE--Passengers are allowed a weight of 200 pounds GROSS including hand baggage, excess charged at $5.00 per 100 pounds, minimum charge 25 cents. EXPRESS RATES, for packages, suit cases, mail matter, etc., $5.00 per hundred pounds, minimum charge 25 cents. Express carried from hangar to hangar only, delivery and receipt by shipper.

Tickets on Sale at Hangars or

"THE HOLE IN THE WALL"
273 Central Avenue

The St Petersburg-Tampa Airboat Line operated the world's first airline service with aeroplanes from 1 January 1914 for four months. Its Benoist flying boat carried a single passenger on each twice-daily flight, at a fare of $5.00, including hand baggage.

The automatic pilot, to ensure safer, smoother flight, was pioneered by Dr Elmer Sperry, who invented the gyro-stabiliser fitted to this Curtiss flying boat in 1913. His son Lawrence demonstrated the device dramatically in the following year, when he won a 50,000 franc Safety Prize by flying the aircraft low over Paris, with his hands off the controls and his passenger standing between the wings.

Tony Jannus and his passenger take off on the first scheduled operation by the St Petersburg-Tampa Airboat Line on 1 January 1914. Two 75hp Roberts engines enabled the Benoist flying boat to offer a flying time of twenty minutes for the twenty mile route over Tampa Bay, Florida, compared with a thirty-six mile journey by road. About 1,200 passengers were carried in four months. The outbreak of the First World War in August prevented any further attempts to organise an airline for aeroplane passenger services until 1919.

Three
Air War 1914-1918

An Avro 500 and Blériot monoplane, with Henri Farmans to the rear, at the RFC's Central Flying School, Upavon, in early 1914. The establishment of this centre for basic flying training, two years earlier, had been a brilliant idea. During the 1914-1918 War, it adopted training methods that set the standard for the world.

Less happy had been a decision to standardise on B.E.2 biplanes as the RFC's operational equipment. This B.E.2a was developed from the B.E.1, designed at the resurgent Aircraft Factory by Geoffrey de Havilland. Reconnaissance was envisaged as the primary duty of military aircraft and few were armed, apart from a rifle, pistol or sporting gun carried by some airmen in the hope of a lucky hit on any enemy they met.

Previous page: This painting by Kenneth McDonough depicts Caproni three-engined strategic bombers of the Italian Army Air Service crossing the Alps on their way to targets in Austria. Muffled against intense cold in the icy slipstream, the gunners on platforms behind the top wing were among the bravest of all aircrew in the first great air war.

Most formidable military aircraft when the war began were Germany's Zeppelin airships, capable of bombing as well as reconnaissance. In August 1914, eleven Zeppelins were available and more were under construction. The German Military Aviation Service had 258 aircraft. The British and French had a total of 219 aircraft on the Western Front, of which the RFC contributed sixty-three. When they crossed the Channel, they were ordered to ram any Zeppelin they encountered on the way.

A Morane-Saulnier Type L monoplane of the kind in which Flt Sub-Lt R.A.J. Warneford of No.1 Squadron, RNAS, destroyed Zeppelin LZ.37 over Bruges on 7 June 1915. Diving from 11,000ft, he dropped six 20lb bombs on the airship, which exploded in flames. Warneford was awarded the Victoria Cross for this first victory over a Zeppelin.

21 November 1914.The first strategic bombing raid in history by a formation of aircraft was made by Sqn Cdr E.F. Briggs, Flt Lt S.V. Sippé and Flt Cdr J.T. Babington of the RNAS in these three Avro 504s, each carrying four 20lb bombs. In an effort to reduce the Zeppelin threat, they flew 125 miles from their base at Belfort near the Franco-Swiss border to the airship sheds at Friedrichshafen in Germany, where they damaged LZ.32 (L.7) in its shed and destroyed the gasworks. Hit by defending gunfire, Briggs was taken prisoner, while the others returned.

Nationality markings, like the Union flag on this unarmed Bristol Scout C of the RNAS, were quickly added when it became clear that soldiers on the ground often fired at any aeroplane that came within range. Germany's iron cross insignia was adopted in September 1914; the British flag followed from 26 October, replaced by red, white and blue roundels on 11 December.

This postcard showing Maurice Farman Srs 11 reconnaissance aircraft of a Belgian squadron was sent by Pte Victor Taylor, a young soldier on the Western Front, to his parents in England. France supplied many aircraft to Allied air forces throughout the war, and the first armed RFC aircraft to appear at a combat base was a similar Srs 11 Shorthorn of No.4 Squadron, fitted with a Lewis machine-gun.

Ungainly Voisin 'chicken-coop' pusher biplanes served throughout the war. In 1914 there was no known way of firing a machine-gun forward through the spinning propeller blades of an aircraft with a front engine. The first victory in air combat was achieved on 5 October by Sgt Joseph Frantz and Cpl Quénault of the French Escadrille VB24 when they shot down a German two-seater, near Reims, with a gun mounted on the nose of their Voisin III. This late-model Voisin X had a 37mm Hotchkiss cannon on the nose and could carry 660lb of bombs.

Aerial warfare began in earnest when the Fokker company perfected interrupter gear that timed bullets to pass between the propeller blades of its Eindecker series of monoplane fighters. Only 425 were built, but they almost shot the Allied air forces from the sky in ten months from August 1915. Germany's first great fighter ace Max Immelmann, seen here in the cockpit, claimed fifteen victories in that time. A 100hp engine gave the Eindecker a top speed of 83mph.

The main victims of what became known as the 'Fokker Scourge' of 1915-1916 were the RFC's B.E.2cs. Changes to the wings had made them so stable during reconnaissance missions that they lacked manoeuvrability to elude the Eindeckers. Their gunner, between the wings, had no clear field of fire to defend them. This B.E.2c of No.4 Squadron was based at Allonville.

The most important duty of the first fighter pilots was to destroy enemy reconnaissance aircraft that were exerting a major influence on the land battle. More fighters were then needed to defend the reconnaissance patrols and fighter-to-fighter combat became ever more fierce. The first Vickers aircraft designed for air fighting were given the unofficial name 'Gunbus'. The F.B.5 version shown had a combat speed of only 50-55mph, making its front gunner ineffective. It was left to the later pusher-engined D.H.2 and F.E.2b, with a front gun, and the French Nieuport Baby, with a gun above the top wing, to end the scourge of the Eindeckers. The availability of interrupter gear then made possible a formidable new generation of single-seat fighters such as the Sopwith Pup and Triplane.

The B.E.2c was replaced by the far superior R.E.8, with a rear gunner behind the pilot. The RFC received 2,262 for reconnaissance and the increasingly important task of flying elliptical patterns to observe and correct the fire of Allied artillery.

The first heavy bombers to enter service were four-engined Sikorsky Ilya Mourometz aircraft of the Russian Czar's Squadron of Flying Ships, from 15 February 1915. The Germans developed similar aircraft to replace Zeppelins which had begun bombing targets in England in January 1915 but suffered increasing losses in bad weather and from aircraft firing incendiary ammunition.

Aeroplanes began to play an important part in the war at sea on 15 August 1915 when a Short 184 seaplane made the first successful torpedo attack from the air against a Turkish steamer. Initially, the 184s had to be lowered on to the water from seaplane carriers, and some were lost when their floats broke up in rough seas.

Although Sopwith Pups had adequate performance to take off from a short deck on seaplane carriers, they had to alight on the water afterwards. Major progress was made on 2 August 1917, when Sqn Cdr E.H. Dunning side-slipped his Pup on to the short forward deck of HMS *Furious* while it was under way. When he tried to repeat the landing he went over the side and was drowned, but *Furious* was rebuilt with a landing deck aft to become the first genuine aircraft carrier.

The Sopwith 1½-Strutter was the first two-seat fighter, with a fixed front gun and a rear gunner, to supplement single-seaters like the Pup on land and at sea. This one is taking off from a platform built over a gun turret on the battle cruiser *Australia*. Two 65lb bombs could be carried for anti-submarine patrol.

The large Felixstowe F.2A flying boats used by the RNAS for long-range anti-submarine and anti-Zeppelin patrols combined the wings of the American Curtiss H.12 with an advanced hull designed by Sqn Cdr John Porte. In their first five months on the octagonal 'Spider Web' patrol area in the North Sea in 1917, they sank four German U-boats. Three Zeppelins were also destroyed by RNAS flying boats. On 4 June 1918, three F.2As were attacked by fourteen German seaplanes and shot down six of the enemy without loss to themselves. The F.2A was powered by two 345hp Rolls-Royce Eagle VIII engines, carried a crew of four, and was armed with up to seven guns and two 230lb bombs.

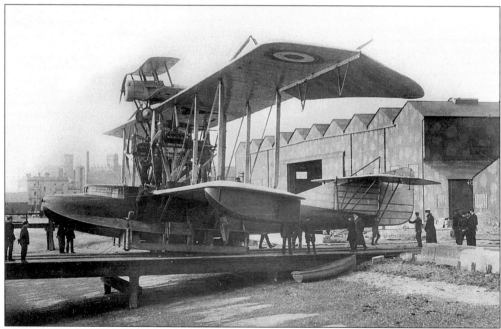

A Bristol Scout was carried into the air and launched from the prototype Porte Baby three-engined flying boat on 17 May 1916, in an experiment to find a quicker way of getting a fighter within striking distance of a Zeppelin. Although not repeated by the RNAS, the concept was revived two decades later for the Short-Mayo composite aircraft that still holds the world distance record for seaplanes.

Tethered kite balloons, sent up to enable observers to report enemy troop movements, had their origin in 1794. The First World War variety, filled with hydrogen, stabilised by fins, and manned by a soldier with a field telephone, made important targets for fighter pilots. Until incendiary ammunition became available, aircraft like this French Caudron G.IV could attack them from close range (under 400ft) with electrically-fired rockets. The balloon observers were provided with parachutes, and a few German combat pilots followed their lead.

When Zeppelins became increasingly vulnerable, their strategic attack mission was taken over by bombers. London suffered its first daylight raid on 13 June 1917, when fourteen Gothas killed 162 people and injured 432 more. Ninety-two British pilots attempted to intercept them, without success. The British authorities issued these illustrations of a Gotha as a recognition aid, and defences slowly improved. The enemy switched to night bombing on 2 September. On 19-20 May 1918, seven of the forty-three aircraft despatched against London and Dover were destroyed and the Germans announced that no more raids would be made on London or Paris. Aeroplane attacks on Britain had killed 857 persons and injured 2,058, for the expenditure of 2,772 bombs weighing a total of 196 tons.

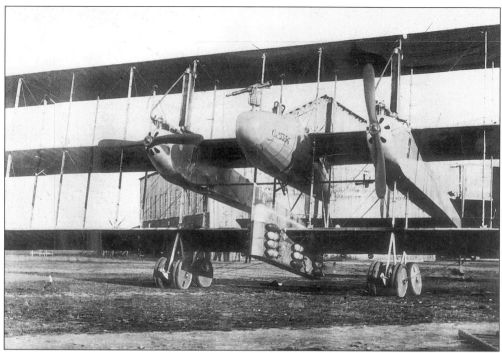

The success of Italy's three-engined Caproni bombers (pages 38-39) encouraged development of the huge Caproni Ca 40 series of twin-engined triplanes, spanning nearly 100ft. Two pilots sat in the central nacelle, with a gunner in the nose and a further gun position in each tailboom. Up to 3,900lb of small bombs were carried on a pannier beneath the crew nacelle. The Ca 40 series could fly for seven hours at 87mph.

The RFC's D.H.4, shown here with a Nieuport Baby escort fighter, was probably the best day bomber of the war. After America entered the war, in April 1917, nearly 5,000 were built in the USA.

The German Junkers J I armoured biplane was one of the most advanced designs of 1914-1918. The 200hp Benz engine and two crew were enclosed in a capsule of 5mm chrome-nickel sheet steel. The all-metal wings, with 2mm corrugated dural skin, were cantilever except for centre-section support struts. J Is entered service in late 1917 and were flown at low altitude, reporting the position of enemy and friendly troops by radio and by dropping message bags. Their crews also dropped ammunition and rations to exposed German front-line troops. Armament comprised two fixed and one observer-operated machine-guns.

In 1917, Lt Col Robert Smith-Barry changed the pattern of military air training for all time. He told the authorities that newly-trained pilots sent to France were mere 'Fokker fodder' and was allowed to set up a School of Special Flying at Gosport to teach flying instructors how to produce competent combat pilots. Instructors in the front cockpit of his dual-control Avro 504s were able to talk to their pupils through a 'telephone' tube while teaching them, so that whatever position they found themselves in during combat, even a dreaded spin, they had learned how to get out of it. Smith-Barry's methods proved so successful that the Central Flying School was reconstituted as an RAF centre for flying instructors that would be copied and attract pupils from all over the world, to the present day.

The most successful fighter of the First World War was the Sopwith Camel. When fitted with a 130hp Clerget engine, this aircraft could fly at 108mph. Some pilots died when the torque of this big rotary flicked them into a vicious right-hand spin. Those that mastered its superb manoeuvrability shot down 1,294 enemy aircraft with the twin Vickers guns.

The Fokker Dr I triplane is best remembered as the favourite mount of Germany's 'Red Baron', Manfred von Richthofen, who claimed the war's highest total of eighty combat victories. It was designed by Reinhold Platz as a result of the success of Sopwith Triplanes and, with a span of only 23ft 7in, shared the agility of the British fighter. However, only 320 were built between 1917 and 1918. After that, the triplane configuration was generally rejected in favour of the well-proven and sturdy braced biplane.

German fighter pilots flew garishly-painted aircraft during the later war years, leading to British identification of *Geschwader 1* as von Richthofen's 'Air Circus'. His preference for an overall blood red finish is part legend, but these Albatros D Vs at Favreuil were fairly typical.

S.E.5a single-seat fighters of A Flight, No.29 Squadron RAF, on 18 August 1918. Like other designs from the Royal Aircraft Factory, the S.E.5a was manufactured by private industry, usually with a 200hp French-designed Hispano-Suiza or a Wolseley development of the same engine known as the Viper. It had a speed of 117mph and was flown by many of Britain's famous aces, including Mannock, Bishop and McCudden.

Another of Reinhold Platz's single-seat fighters, the Fokker D VII entered service in April 1918 with alternative 160hp Mercedes and 185hp BMW engine. With a speed of 116mph and exceptional manoeuvrability, it became so respected by the Allies that Article IV of the Armistice Agreement, listing items that had to be handed over to the victorious Allies, noted 'especially all first-line machines of the D VII type', a unique feature of such a document.

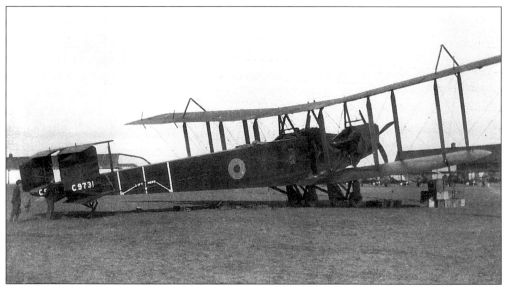

Bombing entered a new dimension when the Independent Force was formed within the newly constituted Royal Air Force on 6 June 1918, with the sole task of waging a sustained strategic attack on German targets. Its spearhead eventually comprised seven squadrons of Handley Page O/400s, powered by two 360hp Rolls-Royce Eagle engines that gave them a speed of 97mph and an endurance of eight hours carrying up to 2,000lb of bombs, including big 1,650-pounders. They proved so effective in night operations that the leader of the Independent Force, General Hugh (later Marshal of the Royal Air Force Viscount) Trenchard, became a lifelong advocate of air attack.

Sopwith was one of the few companies that continued to build military aircraft after the Armistice of November 1918. These Salamander single-seat armoured ground attack aircraft and Snipe single-seat fighters at its Ham works, near Kingston upon Thames, in December 1918, were completed for service with the post-war Royal Air Force.

The First World War ended on 11 November 1918. Its cost had been utterly devastating, its impact on aviation progress questionable. Almost every type of air warfare known today had been developed, and strategists already foresaw that entire cities might be wiped off the map by air attack if the description of 1914-1918 as 'the war to end wars' proved to be wrong. But was this progress?

The Royal Flying Corps had realized quickly that it could not rely on the Royal Aircraft Factory to design all the aeroplanes that it needed. Initially, it survived by accepting aircraft from France and others like the Sopwith Pup and Triplane that had been designed privately for the Royal Naval Air Service. By 1918, the Royal Aircraft Factory had been renamed the Royal Aircraft Establishment, with the task of providing a research centre on behalf of the private manufacturers who would be responsible for all future design and production.

British factories had delivered 55,093 airframes during the war years; 67,982 had been built in France, 47,637 in Germany and about 20,000 in Italy. In the nineteen months since it entered combat, the US had demonstrated its immense productive capability by building 15,000 aircraft. However, the only US designs used in combat were the big Curtiss flying boats. US pilots in France flew mostly D.H.4 bombers, many built in America, and French Nieuport and SPAD fighters. When the Armistice was signed, the Royal Air Force had 22,171 aeroplanes in service and in store; the Germans had about 20,000 and the French more than 15,000. Most had fabric-covered wood structure, little different from the best aeroplanes of 1914. The only real progress had been made by engine builders like Rolls-Royce, Hispano and Mercedes, whose products had greatly increased power and reliability.

Those who hoped for a post-war boom in civil flying were quickly disillusioned. Most production contracts were cancelled overnight, with little hope of new orders as the world was awash with surplus combat and training aircraft. Germany was forbidden by the Versailles Treaty to build new military aeroplanes. Russia's embryo industry had virtually died after the Bolshevik Revolution. It was left to a handful of adventurers to open up the air routes of the future, and to barnstormers in war-weary training aircraft to persuade the public that flying was not just for heroes by offering joyrides for a few shillings or dollars a time.

Four
A Limitless Horizon

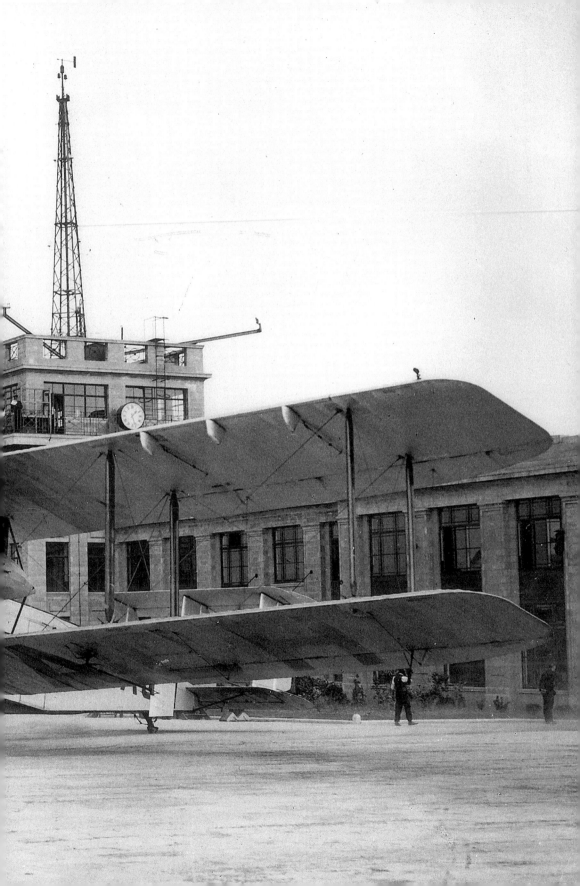

Despite the post-war depression, Germany was first to authorise civil airline operations, on 8 January 1919. The company which began the world's first sustained daily passenger service with aeroplanes, on 5 February, was Deutsche Luft Reederei, flying between Berlin and Weimar via Leipzig. Well muffled against the cold of the open cockpit, and clasping hands for courage, this couple is preparing for take-off in a converted LVG C.VI wartime reconnaissance aircraft.

The first Atlantic crossing by air was made by the US Navy/Curtiss flying boat NC-4. It took off from Trepassy Bay, Newfoundland, on 16 May 1919, as one of a flight of three NCs commanded by Cdr John H. Towers. Only NC-4 completed the 2,475 mile journey to the Tagus river, off Lisbon in Portugal, via two stops in the Azores, on 27 May, before flying on to Plymouth on 31 May.

Previous page: An Armstrong Whitworth Argosy twenty-passenger airliner of Imperial Airways in front of the famous control tower at Croydon Airport, London. Its cruising speed of 90-95mph gave time for the airline to serve buffet bar meals on its *Silver Wing* luxury lunchtime flights between Croydon and Le Bourget Airport, Paris.

This photograph of the left-hand pilot's cockpit of the NC-4 flying boat emphasises how few flying and navigation instruments were available to those who set out to cross the Atlantic by air for the first time in 1919.

Before the First World War no aircraft was capable of winning a *Daily Mail* prize of £10,000 for the first successful non-stop flight across the North Atlantic. Several pilots decided to make attempts in 1919. The prize was won by Capt. John Alcock and Lt Arthur Whitten Brown, who, on 14 June, took off from St John's, Newfoundland, in a Vickers Vimy bomber with two 350hp Rolls-Royce Eagle engines. They flew for sixteen hours twenty-seven minutes to Clifden, County Galway, Ireland, where they landed in a bog and almost overturned. Both were knighted for their achievement.

Production of aircraft specifically for commercial airline use began with the German Junkers F 13, first flown on 25 June 1919. It was of all-metal construction, with the company's 'trademark' corrugated metal skin. A 240hp BMW engine enabled it to carry two crew and four passengers at 85mph. Many hundreds were built for worldwide use.

25 August 1919. The world's first scheduled daily international commercial airline service was flown in a DH.4A converted bomber of Aircraft Transport & Travel Ltd, from Hounslow to Le Bourget, by Lt E.H. Lawford. He carried one passenger, George Stevenson-Reece, and a cargo of newspapers, leather, grouse and Devonshire cream. Later in the day, Cyril Patteson flew the same route in this D.H.16 with four passengers, in two hours and thirty minutes. The one-way fare was £21.

The first flight between the UK and Australia was made in a Vimy by Australian brothers, Capt. Ross Smith and Lt Keith Smith, with two crew, who flew 11,294 miles from Hounslow to Darwin between 12 November and 10 December 1919, in a flying time of 135 hours 55 minutes. They won an Australian government prize of £10,000 and received knighthoods. Before their success, sceptics suggested that the registration of the Vimy, G-EAOU, stood for 'God 'Elp All Of Us'.

1 February 1920. Capt. J.F. Godman of the Somali Camel Corps is removed from a converted D.H.9 bomber at Eil dur Elan after the first aero-medical flight by an RAF air ambulance.

Years ahead of its time, Oswald Short's Silver Streak was the first all-metal aeroplane with a monocoque fuselage. Powered by a 240hp Siddeley Puma engine, it began life as a single-seater with space forward of the cockpit for 400lb of cargo or mail. Before it flew, on 20 August 1920, it was converted into a two-seater and bought by the Air Ministry for £4,500. However, little interest in monocoque construction was shown officially until the mid-1930s.

Jack Knight was the hero of the US Post Office's first experimental transcontinental air mail flight. He took over the ex-military D.H.4M at North Platte, Nebraska, after it had been flown by a succession of pilots from San Francisco, on 22 February 1921. When he landed at Omaha, he discovered that the man scheduled to fly the next stage had decided that the weather was too bad to carry on. Although tired, Knight continued the flight through the dark to Chicago over unfamiliar territory, enabling other pilots to complete the service to New York in a total elapsed time of thirty-three hours and twenty minutes. He was hailed as the saviour of the air mail operation. A system of lighting to permit safe night flying over part of the route was installed in 1923, and a regular 2,600 mile transcontinental mail service began on 1 July 1924. This paved the way for Western Air Express to operate the first sustained US passenger service, between Salt Lake City and Los Angeles, with Douglas M-2s, from 23 May 1926.

As commander of US Air Service units on the Western Front in the summer of 1918, General William (Billy) Mitchell found himself with forty-nine squadrons of aircraft, half of them American, plus more than forty French squadrons under his control and nine bombing squadrons of the RAF Independent Force ready to co-operate with him. He flung an unprecedented fleet of 1,481 aircraft against the Germans during the successful battle for the St Mihiel salient. Thereafter a fierce proponent of all-out air power, he attempted to prove that the biggest battleships were vulnerable to air attack by using Martin MB-2 bombers to sink old German and US warships at sea between 1921 and 1923. Crossing swords with the US military hierarchy, he was court-martialled and suspended from duty in 1925. Twenty years later, after his death, he was restored to service with the rank of Major General and awarded the Congressional Medal of Honor.

At the Cairo Conference in 1922, another great advocate of air power, Britain's Chief of Air Staff, Major General Sir Hugh (later Marshal of the Royal Air Force Viscount) Trenchard, persuaded his government to replace most army units that were keeping the peace in Iraq with eight RAF squadrons. So began the policy of air control, which eventually maintained an uneasy peace throughout much of the Middle East and the north-west frontier of India by deterring dissident tribesmen and bombing their villages only after warnings that saved countless lives on each side. Typical of the aircraft employed initially was this D.H.9A, a modification by Westland of the First World War D.H.9 bomber with a 400hp American Liberty engine.

In 1921, in response to a Japanese request to the UK government for help in organising, training and advising its Navy Air Service, a British Air Mission, under Col. The Master of Sempill, began the task with fifty Gloster Sparrowhawk fighters. One of them is shown here being hoisted into position on to the gun turret launch platform of a Japanese warship. How efficiently the Japanese Navy responded to its early training was to be demonstrated in December 1941.

In an effort to make the US public air-minded, many ex-military pilots bought war-surplus Curtiss 'Jenny' trainers and barnstormed with them across America. Hair-raising displays of aerobatics and wing-walking, including stunts such as climbing from one aircraft to another, were interspersed with joyrides for members of the crowd brave enough to part with a few dollars.

International seaplane contests for the Schneider Trophy resumed in 1919. The Curtiss CR-3, in which Lt David Rittenhouse of the US Navy won in 1923 at Cowes in the UK, at a speed of 177.38mph, was an eye-opener. Its closely-cowled 450hp Curtiss D-12 engine led to design of the RAF's Fairey Fox, first with a similar engine that advanced the speed of RAF day bombers by more than 35% and then with a 480hp Rolls-Royce Kestrel which pointed the way to the famous Merlin, the outstanding aero-engine of the Second World War.

9 January 1923. The first flight of Juan de la Cierva's C-4 Autogiro at Madrid, Spain, marked the most important early milestone in rotating-wing flight. Although its rotor was unpowered, it offered hope of improved safety by eliminating long take-off and landing runs, making possible the practical helicopter in the 1930s.

In-flight refuelling, to increase aircraft range, was another key technique of the future demonstrated successfully in 1923. Repeated refuellings by a D.H.4B-1 'flying tanker' enabled Lts Lowell H. Smith and John P. Richter of the US Air Service to remain airborne for a record thirty-seven hours and fifteen minutes in their D.H.4, over San Diego on 27 and 28 August.

Two Douglas DWC World Cruisers of the US Army Air Service photographed at Croydon. They were part of a flight of four that took off from Seattle on 6 April 1924 in an attempt to make the first successful round-the-world flight. Named after US cities, *Seattle* hit a mountain in Alaska, while *Boston* force-landed in the Atlantic. With interchangeable wheels and floats for different stages of the flight, *Chicago* and *New Orleans* landed back at Seattle on 28 September after a 27,553 mile flight over twenty-eight countries.

Airliner pilots of the 1920s sat in open cockpits. Passengers, like those who flew in this Handley Page W.10 of Imperial Airways, had wicker seats in a spartan enclosed cabin, with overhead luggage racks and a ceiling chart of the route between Croydon and Le Bourget supplied by BP Aviation Spirit. The state-subsidised Imperial Airways had been formed on 31 March 1924 by merging the earlier Handley Page, Instone, Daimler and British Marine Air Navigation airlines.

Alan Cobham surveyed air routes to the farthest parts of the British Empire, on behalf of Imperial Airways, in this D.H.50 with interchangeable wheels and floats. His flights to Capetown and back and to Australia and back in 1925-1926 gained him a knighthood. He made a 23,000 mile circuit of Africa in 1927 in a Short Singapore flying-boat, organised the National Aviation Day 'air circus' that toured the British Isles between 1932 and 1935, and perfected the modern technique of probe-and-drogue air-to-air refuelling.

The trimotor Fokker *Josephine Ford*, shown here in the Ford Museum at Dearborn, Michigan, was used by Lt Cdr (later Rear-Admiral) Richard Byrd for the first flight over the North Pole on 9 May 1926, piloted by Floyd Bennett. After Bennett died, Byrd made the first flight over the South Pole on 29 November 1929 in the Ford Trimotor *Floyd Bennett*, piloted by Bernt Balchen, one of the greatest of all Arctic flyers.

The 24-year-old American Charles Lindbergh made the first non-stop New York-Paris flight in this small Ryan monoplane *Spirit of St Louis* on 20-21 May 1927. Flying alone, he covered the 3,610 miles in thirty-three hours and thirty-nine minutes, without radio and with a periscope to see forward around the large fuel tank that filled the space between the 220hp engine and his seat. The achievement gained him a $25,000 prize, international fame and appointment as Technical Advisor to the newly-formed Pan American Airways, set to become the US flagship airline.

The contests for the Schneider Trophy reached their climax between 1927 and 1931, when Britain's succession of Supermarine S.5, S.6 and S.6B seaplanes beat fierce international competition to win the Trophy outright with victories in three consecutive bi-annual meetings. The pilots were members of the Royal Air Force. Design experience gained with R.J. Mitchell's superb all-metal airframes and the 2,300hp Rolls-Royce engine of the S.6B had a major influence on the development of his later Spitfire fighter. S.5 N219, winner in 1927, is shown taxiing past one of Italy's Macchis while serving as a training aircraft in 1929. An S.6B, flown by Flt Lt G.H. Stainforth, became the first aeroplane to exceed 400mph when it set a world speed record of 406.94mph on 29 September 1931.

To compete with the *Silver Wing* lunchtime service offered on Armstrong Whitworth Argosies of Imperial Airways from 1 May 1927, Air Union, a predecessor of Air France, refurnished two of its twelve-passenger *Rayon d'Or* (Golden Ray) LeO 213s as LeO 212 restaurant aircraft. Airline passenger service entered a new era.

Small freight being loaded on board one of Air Union's twin-engined LeO 21s in front of the famous Croydon control tower, opened as part of a new terminal in January 1928.

50th Anniversary
Royal Flying Doctor Service
First Day of Issue   •   15th May 1978

On the other side of the globe, Australia inaugurated its pioneer Flying Doctor Service on 15 May 1928 with the D.H.50 *Victory*, adapted to carry two stretchers. The concept of spreading 'a mantle of safety' by air over the vast, inaccessible outback was suggested by the Rev. John Flynn, using the joint services of the Australian Inland Mission and the national airline QANTAS. When the outback stations were connected to the Service's HQ by radio, a pattern was established for the world.

During a tribal rebellion in Afghanistan at the end of 1928, the British Legation in Kabul was cut off from the rest of the city. In response to a request from Sir Francis Humphrys, the British Commissioner, the RAF mounted the first major airlift in history. Between 23 December 1928 and 25 February 1929, squadrons of D.H.9As and Bristol F.2bs from India, Victoria transports of No.70 Squadron from Iraq and a single Handley Page Hinaidi evacuated 586 civilians and nearly 25,000lb of baggage from Kabul over 10,000ft mountains during one of the severest winters on record, flying a total of 28,160 miles. Passengers are seen leaving a Victoria at Risalpur, India.

With few major airports worldwide, flying-boats were regarded as the most appropriate aircraft for use on long over-water routes when airlines began to expand their networks. Largest of its time was Germany's Dornier Do X, completed at Altenrhein on the Swiss shore of Lake Constance. When fitted with twelve 600hp Curtiss Conqueror engines, it spanned 157ft 5¾in, had a maximum take-off weight of 123,457lb, and was designed to carry between sixty-nine and 100 passengers for 1,056 miles at 118mph. The prototype flew on 25 July 1929 and made a ten-month tour from Germany to New York, via Rio, in 1930-1931. Two more were delivered to an Italian airline but never entered service.

The short upper deck of the Do X housed the flight deck for two pilots, a captain's cabin and navigation room, an engine control room and the radio cabin. Harvey Brewton, chief engineer on the transatlantic flight, is shown in the engine room.

British heroine of the 1930s was Amy Johnson, who made the first solo flight by a woman from England to Australia in the D.H.60G Gipsy Moth *Jason* between 5 and 24 May 1930. Since the prototype of Geoffrey de Havilland's little two-seat Moth flew, on 22 February 1925, it had become a worldwide success. Moths of various kinds were built in thousands, in Australia, Finland, France, the USA, Canada and Norway in addition to the UK, making possible the start of the flying club movement. From 1928, they even had their own engine, the 100/120hp de Havilland Gipsy, with which the D.H.60G cost £650.

Airline stewardesses made their debut on 15 May 1930, when a young nurse named Ellen Church persuaded the management of Boeing Air Transport (later part of United Air Lines) to let her handle cabin service on a flight between San Francisco and Cheyenne, Wyoming. Initial pilot protests were dropped after her insistence on a diversion saved the life of a seriously ill passenger, and Ellen Church (third from left) was allowed to recruit these seven additional stewardesses, all trained nurses.

Introduction by Imperial Airways of eight four-engined Handley Page H.P.42/45 four-engined airliners, from June 1931, provided an enclosed cockpit for the pilots at last. Leather flying suits, helmets and goggles gave way to smart uniforms and peaked caps. The H.P.42s' cruising speed was still under 100mph, but these famous aircraft never hurt a passenger until one of them disappeared on a Second World War flight in the Middle East.

Except for photographs issued for propaganda purposes, little was known about aviation development in Russia during the inter-war years. Only now can the true qualities of designers like Andrei Tupolev be appreciated. His ungainly TB-3s of the early 1930s were the first four-engined cantilever monoplane bombers; but the policies and purges of Stalin made Soviet strategic air power ineffective by the time of the Second World War.

National prestige was all-important to the Fascist rulers of Italy and Germany in the 1930s, In 1931, General Italo Balbo, the Italian Air Minister, led twelve Savoia-Marchetti S.55 flying-boats on the first formation flight across the South Atlantic from Rome to Brazil. Two years later, he led twenty-four of the flying-boats across the North Atlantic, to Chicago and back. Although each flight cost lives, the growing reliability and possibilities of aviation were apparent to all.

Since 1909, Professor Hugo Junkers had believed that one day huge flying-wing airliners would be able to carry up to 1,000 people across the North Atlantic in $1\frac{1}{2}$ days. The nearest he came to realizing his dream was when his company built two G 38s between 1928 and 1931. In their final form, each carried seven crew and thirty-four passengers on two decks. There were small cabins, with forward-facing windows, in the nose and in the leading-edge of each wing centre-section, a smoking cabin, buffet, two toilets and a washroom. The second G 38 was operated for several years by Lufthansa.

After the Moth, the aircraft that did most to get private flyers into the air was probably the Cub. The 1930 prototype, known as the Taylor E-2, is shown with its designer, C.G. Taylor, and test pilot Bud Havens. It had two seats in tandem in an open cockpit and was powered by a 40hp Salmson engine. After the Taylor Aircraft Company had been bought by W.T. Piper, the E-2 was developed into the less angular J-2 with an enclosed cockpit, 37/40hp Continental engine and range of 210 miles at 70mph. Renamed the Piper Cub, it became the first product of the Piper Aircraft Corporation in 1937.

In the 1930s, many unique aeroplanes were designed to compete in the US National Air Races. None were more famous than the two Gee Bee Super Sportsters, with the smallest possible airframe that could be built around a 730hp Pratt & Whitney engine. Major James H. (Jimmy) Doolittle flew one of them at 294mph in 1932. Both eventually crashed, killing other pilots.

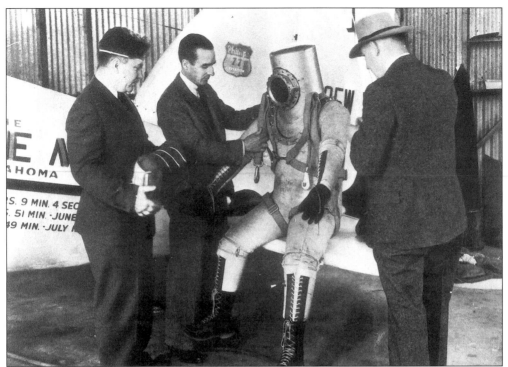

Wiley Post (left) made two round-the-world record flights in the Lockheed Vega *Winnie Mae*, the first with navigator Harold Gatty in 1931, followed by the first-ever solo circumnavigation in 1933. He then pioneered the development of this early pressure suit during high altitude flights in the Vega.

The first flight of the Boeing 247, on 8 February 1933, marked the birth of the modern all-metal airliner with cantilever low wings, twin engines, retractable landing gear, control surface trim tabs, automatic pilot and de-icing equipment. US transcontinental flight time was reduced to under twenty hours with ten passengers. By 1935 United Air Lines' basic 155mph Model 247s had been uprated to this 247D standard, with geared 550hp Pratt & Whitney Wasp engines, controllable-pitch propellers and a cruising speed of 189mph.

The first flights over Mount Everest, the highest point on Earth, were made on 3 April 1933 by the Marquis of Clydesdale in the Westland PV.3 and Flt Lt D.F. McIntyre in a Westland Wallace, each with one passenger. The originator of the expedition, Col. Stewart Blacker, took this photograph of the PV.3 approaching the summit at 34,000ft, from the enclosed rear cabin of the Wallace. Both pilots sat in open cockpits!

This Dornier Wal flying boat of Lufthansa inaugurated the first regular transatlantic mail service between Bathurst in Gambia and Natal in Brazil on 3 February 1934. It refuelled in mid-Atlantic on board the depot ship *Westfalen*, from which it was catapulted on the final stage of the flight. The service was maintained, with Blohm & Voss Ha 139 seaplanes from 1938, until the outbreak of the Second World War.

Sir Alan Cobham's National Aviation Day displays provided the public with all the excitement of the old barnstorming era and the opportunity to get a first taste of flying with 'ten-bob joyrides' in veteran Avro 504s, Moths and twin-engined airliners. Some 60% of the RAF's Second World War pilots are believed to have flown for the first time with Cobham's 'air circus' and during his earlier tour to promote the opening of municipal aerodromes between 1929 and 1935.

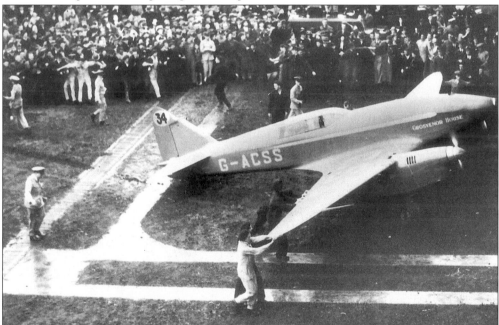

The de Havilland company built three D.H.88 Comet two-seat racing aircraft, each with two 230hp Gipsy Six engines, to compete in the MacRobertson trans-world air race between England and Australia in October 1934, marking the centenary of the founding of the State of Victoria. Built of wood and of exceptionally clean design, Comet G-ACSS *Grosvenor House*, flown by C.W.A. Scott and Tom Campbell Black, won the race by landing in Melbourne seventy hours fifty-four minutes and eighteen seconds after taking off from Mildenhall in Suffolk. The globe had been spanned in under three days for the first time.

Hart two-seat day bombers of No.33 Squadron, RAF. Since the time of the Curtiss D-12 engine, British military designers had preferred the clean lines made possible by liquid-cooled in-line power plants. Hawker Aircraft's great Chief Designer, Sydney Camm, chose 485/640hp Rolls-Royce Kestrels for the many variants and developments of the Hart, and the single-seat Fury fighter, which outnumbered all other operational types in the Royal Air Force during the 1930s.

US designers generally preferred air-cooled radial engines, although this resulted in a large 'draggy' frontal area. The 950hp Wright R-1820 and retractable landing gear of these Grumman F3F-2s of US Marine Corps Squadron VMF-2 gave them a top speed of 260mph. They had the then-standard US fighter armament of two machine-guns.

The Tupolev ANT-20, flying over Red Square in Moscow, was the giant of its day, with a span of 206ft 8in, maximum weight of 92,592lb and eight 900hp engines. Built for the Soviet *Agiteskadrilya* (propaganda squadron), it could carry seventy-two passengers and contained a printing press, cinema, darkroom and telephone system, with external loudspeakers and underwing electric lamps to display slogans. It was lost on 18 May 1935, with forty-five occupants, when the pilot of an escorting I-5 fighter collided with the ANT-20 while attempting to loop around it.

The German Focke-Wulf Fw 61 helicopter, with twin rotors on outriggers, marked an important step forward. It set eight official records between 1937 and 1939, including speed (76mph), height (11,243ft) and distance (143 miles). Diminutive test pilot Hanna Reitsch even flew one of the two prototypes inside the Deutschlandhalle sports stadium in Berlin in February 1938 to demonstrate its controllability. During the Second World War, it was planned to build 400 larger four-seat Fa 223s each month for the German armed forces, but sixteen out of eighteen completed were destroyed by Allied air attack.

A fourteen-passenger DST (Douglas sleeper transport) of American Airlines being prepared for an overnight flight from Los Angeles to New York. First of the legendary DC-3 series, the DST owed its existence to the fact that the first fifty-nine Boeing 247s had been delivered exclusively to United Air Lines, part-owned by Boeing. Unable to wait while its main competitor was supplied, Trans World Airlines sponsored development of the original Douglas DC-1. This led to the improved DC-2, followed by the DST, first flown on 17 December 1935, and twenty-one to twenty-eight-passenger DC-3 with engines of 1,000 to 1,200hp. Over a twelve-year period, Douglas built 10,654 civil and military aircraft of the DC-3/C-47 series. Another 485 were produced in Japan and some 2,000 similar PS-84/Li-2s in the Soviet Union.

By the mid-1930s, only the Pacific and North Atlantic Oceans still presented major challenges to world airlines. The first trans-Pacific mail service was opened by Pan American Airways on 22 November 1935, using Martin M.130 Clipper flying boats. Journey time from San Francisco to Manila in the Philippines was six days, via Honolulu, Midway Island, Wake Island and Guam. It had been made possible only by establishing bases at the coral atolls of Midway and Wake, made more difficult as Wake had no harbour, vegetation, shelter or, initially, food or fresh water. Passenger services with the forty-eight-passenger M.130s followed from 21 October 1936.

In December 1934, the UK government announced its intention to inaugurate the Empire Air Mail Scheme, under which all letters and postcards would be carried by air throughout all parts of the Empire served by Imperial Airways, at a cost of only 1½ pence per half-ounce. To operate the scheme, Imperial ordered twenty-eight Short S.23 C-class flying boats. The first of them, G-ADHL *Canopus*, flew on 3 July 1936 and entered service less than four months later, equipped to carry twenty-four passengers and 1½ tons of mail. Like *Castor* (above), it remained in service for ten years.

Two S.30 C-class flying boats, named *Cabot* and *Caribou*, were designed with the ability to increase their take-off weight of 48,000lb by a further 5,000lb by refuelling in flight from Handley Page Harrow bombers equipped as tankers by Sir Alan Cobham's Flight Refuelling company. This enabled them to carry a two-ton payload on the first British scheduled North Atlantic air mail service in the summer of 1939. The service used to do eight weekly crossings in each direction until it was stopped by the war. By then, Imperial Airways had become the British Overseas Airways Corporation.

In 1937, a few experimental transatlantic flights between Botwood, Newfoundland, and Foynes were made by Pan American Sikorsky S-42 flying boats and the Imperial Airways C-class *Caledonia* and *Cambria*, fitted with additional fuel tanks. Commercial passenger flights finally became possible from 8 July 1939, when Pan Am's seventy-four-passenger Boeing 314s opened a regular service between New York and Southampton and Marseilles, via Newfoundland, at a return fare of $675. This is one of three 314s passed on to BOAC for wartime use.

It is often forgotten that Deutsche Zeppelin Reederei, of Germany, carried more than 16,000 passengers, mostly over the Atlantic, in the giant airships LZ 127 *Graf Zeppelin* and LZ 129 *Hindenburg*, in standards reminiscent of a great ocean liner. The twenty-passenger LZ 127 began regular operation over the South Atlantic in summer, between Friedrichshafen and Recife (later Rio de Janeiro), in April 1932. The fifty-passenger LZ 129 made ten return flights across the North Atlantic in summer 1936, averaging sixty-five hours westbound and fifty-two hours eastbound, at a single fare of £80. Its accommodation was then increased to seventy-two passengers and fifty-five crew. Sadly, at the end of the first crossing of the new season, on 6 May 1937, it exploded in flames at Lakehurst, New Jersey, with the loss of thirty-five lives. Zeppelin passenger services ended, but LZ 130, shown over one of Germany's world-beating Mercedes racing cars in 1939, made a few clandestine military reconnaissance flights.

First flown on 31 December 1938, the Boeing 307 Stratoliner was little more than a B-17C bomber airframe fitted with a new fuselage of much enlarged circular section. The main difference, however, was that it was pressurized, thus offering its thirty-three airline passengers more comfortable flights above most rough weather for the first time. Three were delivered to Pan American, five to TWA and this one to Howard Hughes, whose intention to fly it round the world was abandoned on the outbreak of war.

Five

Air Power Dominant

Russia's little Polikarpov I-16 was the first low-wing single-seat fighter monoplane with a retractable landing gear to enter service with any air force, in 1935. It had been designed with an enclosed cockpit, but its pilots preferred to fly without the canopy, even at its maximum speed of 283mph. When the Civil War began in Spain, the Soviet Union supplied many combat aircraft to the Republican forces, including I-16s which could outfight early versions of Germany's Messerschmitt Bf 109.

While the Soviet Union supported the Spanish Republicans, Germany and Italy strongly backed General Franco's insurgents. Italian SIAI S.M.81 bombers and Fiat C.R.32 fighters like these were flown by both Italian and Spanish airmen. The devastating raid by Heinkel He 111 bombers and Junkers Ju 52 bomber-transports of Germany's Condor Legion on the Spanish city of Guernica, on 26 April 1937, gave a tragic foretaste of what was to come in the Second World War.

Previous page: Symbols on the nose of RAF Lancaster S for Sugar indicate that it had already completed nearly 100 bombing missions at the time this photograph was taken. Weapons being loaded include a 4,000lb Cookie. Only the Lancaster could carry the 12,000lb Tallboy and 22,000lb Grand Slam 'earthquake bombs', largest high-explosive bombs of the Second World War.

Germany's Heinkel He 178 was the first jet-powered aircraft to fly, on 27 August 1939, with an HeS 3b engine designed by Dr Pabst von Ohain. With the outbreak of war imminent, the flight was kept secret. Maximum speed of the He 178 was only 373mph and, although Heinkel flew its He 280 (the world's first potential jet-fighter) on 2 April 1941, it was not ordered for the Luftwaffe. As a result, no jet combat aircraft, German or Allied, became operational until the second half of 1944 and they played little part in the war.

The Second World War began on 1 September 1939, when Germany launched its *Blitzkrieg* (lightning war) on Poland. The Army was spearheaded by Ju 87 *Stuka* dive-bombers of the Luftwaffe, and the campaign was over in twenty-eight days. The vulnerability of the Ju 87 did not become apparent until it was matched against RAF Hurricanes and Spitfires one year later.

On 3 April 1940, the *Blitzkrieg* was directed against Germany's Northern and Western Front. Denmark was occupied in nine days. The ultimate success of the campaign against Norway was ensured by the availability of 500 Ju 52 transports to fly in parachute troops, other army units and Luftwaffe ground crews. Similar use of Ju 52s won Crete for Germany in mid-1941, but at such high cost that it never again mounted a major airborne invasion. Russia had already pioneered paratroop drops from its TB-3 bomber-transports in the 1930s.

By mid-June 1940, the Netherlands, Belgium and France had been defeated. Winston Churchill warned, 'I expect that the Battle of Britain is about to begin'. The Luftwaffe's Bf 109Es, now based in the conquered nations, prepared to escort huge fleets of bombers over the Channel. Britain's chain of radar stations that would see them coming, allied to a network of Observer Corps posts and reporting centres, was to prove crucial. So was the Bf 109's short endurance, which limited the time it was able to spend defending the bombers.

The Luftwaffe's attack force of more than 1,000 bombers ranged against Britain in August 1940 consisted primarily of Heinkel He 111s, like these crossing the British coast, Dornier Do 17s and Junkers Ju 88s. So many were lost that, after a month, they began switching to night operations, using radio navigation systems and pathfinder aircraft that enabled them to create widespread devastation in London, Coventry, Bristol and other major cities and ports, until the RAF received adequate numbers of Bristol Beaufighters equipped with airborne interception radar. Not until mid-1941 did the night Blitz end, when all possible Luftwaffe units were concentrated for the invasion of Russia.

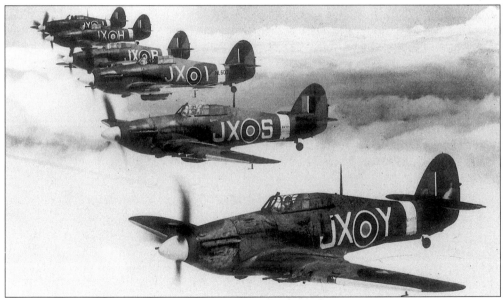

On 11 August 1940, RAF Fighter Command had 704 serviceable aircraft. Most numerous were thirty squadrons of Hurricanes, its first 300mph aircraft and the first with eight machine-guns. Soon supplemented with more squadrons, they destroyed more than 60% of all enemy aircraft shot down in the Battle of Britain. These later Mk IIC Hurricanes of No.1 Squadron have four 20mm cannon. By September 1941 they were dropping 250lb and then 500lb bombs. In the following year Hurricanes added air-to-ground rockets and underwing 40mm guns with which tropicalized squadrons in North Africa destroyed many of Rommel's tanks before the key Battle of El Alamein.

Nineteen squadrons of eight-gun Supermarine Spitfire Mk1s were available on 11 August 1940. They were the fastest aircraft used in the Battle of Britain, with a maximum speed of 355mph. Later versions served throughout the war and after, with progressively improved performance and speeds up to 460mph, as well as armament of four 20mm guns and 1,000lb of bombs or rockets. Others served as unarmed photo-reconnaissance aircraft.

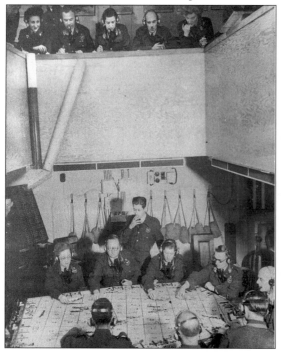

A Royal Observer Corps reporting centre. By receiving reports of all aircraft sighted at its network of posts, plotting them on its Group map table, and passing information to Fighter Command, the Corps supplemented radar thus enabling RAF squadrons to be directed against individual enemy formations as they approached, instead of wasting precious time and fuel on standing patrols. After the Battle of Britain, it was granted the title Royal to mark its contribution to victory.

Aircraft could be – and were – replaced speedily during the war, as losses increased. Trained aircrew were more precious, and air-sea rescue of those who parachuted into the water became an important task. This German He 59B-3 seaplane, initially intended for attack and reconnaissance, is shown picking up men from a dinghy. The RAF began by using Supermarine Walrus amphibians for air-sea rescue, later adapting the Vickers Warwick bomber to parachute an airborne lifeboat to survivors.

The importance of pre-emptive strike was emphasised dramatically on 22 June 1941, the first day of Hitler's invasion of the Soviet Union that began what Russians call the Great Patriotic War. These derelict Polikarpov I-16 and MiG-3 fighters, Tupolev SB bombers and other types symbolise the 1,811 Soviet aircraft that the Luftwaffe destroyed, 1,489 of them on the ground, in a single day, against the loss of thirty-five German aircraft.

As the Germans advanced, the Soviet Union withdrew its aircraft production by rail to factories east of the Urals, in Siberia, during the period between October and December 1941. There it built many of the 108,028 combat aircraft that its air forces received throughout the war. A total of 36,163 of these ground attack Ilyushin Il-2 Shturmoviks played a major role in driving back the enemy with guns, bombs and rockets, their heavy armour enabling them to survive German defensive fire. Many of the 36,000 Yakovlev fighters had wood-covered wings, which helped the Soviet Union to save 30,000 tons of precious aluminium sheet in two and a half years.

From the earliest months of the war, RAF bombers had scattered propaganda leaflets on Germany and the German forces. As 1941 ended, with Russia defending its homeland fiercely, this leaflet recalled Hitler's promise that the war would end in 1941, adding 'In Russia, fallen leaves cover fallen soldiers – and snow covers the leaves which cover fallen soldiers.'

The Luftwaffe's Ju 52s no longer dropped invading paratroops but wore red crosses and evacuated German wounded from Russia in the summer of 1942.

Invasion of England had no longer been practical after the defeat of the Luftwaffe in the Battle of Britain. Now, survival of the UK depended on keeping open the Atlantic sea lanes. German U-boats that devastated British convoys bringing food, weapons and supplies were joined by Focke-Wulf Fw 200 Condor anti-shipping bombers, which sank 363,000 tons of Allied shipping between 1 August 1940 and 9 February 1941 alone.

To combat the Fw 200s, Hurricane fighters were launched from catapult-armed merchant ships (CAM-ships). They claimed only five of the big bombers, and their pilots had to ditch in the sea at the end of a sortie and hope to be picked up. However, the Fw 200s were soon forced to restrict their missions to shadowing convoys and reporting their position by radio.

MV *Empire MacAlpine* was a merchant aircraft carrier (MAC-ship), with a rudimentary flight deck over its loaded cargo hold and a complement of four Fairey Swordfish anti-submarine aircraft. These antiquated biplanes, flown from all types of carrier and from land, sank more enemy shipping, including U-boats, than any other Allied aircraft. They torpedoed and slowed the battleship *Bismarck* so that the Royal Navy could catch and sink it, and devastated much of the Italian fleet in Taranto harbour in November 1940.

Short Sunderland flying boats of RAF Coastal Command became increasingly effective, on a wide variety of duties, as the war progressed. Their defensive armament enabled them to fight off intercepting enemy aircraft with such success that the Luftwaffe nicknamed Sunderlands 'flying porcupines'. Using ASV sea-search radar and depth charges, they sank thirty-one U-boats.

This Japanese photograph shows one of the 360 carrier-based aircraft that attacked the US Pacific Fleet in its home base at Pearl Harbor, Hawaii, on 7 December 1941. Smoke can be seen rising from US warships sunk and damaged during the attack, which brought the USA into the war against Japan and Germany. It signalled the start of Japan's rapid advance through South-east Asia.

The US Navy's eight aircraft carriers were at sea when Pearl Harbor was attacked. Within three days, aircraft from USS *Enterprise* sank a Japanese submarine. On 18 April 1942, these sixteen US Army Air Force B-25 Mitchells, never intended for deck flying, took off from USS *Hornet* for an 800-mile flight to Japan as an indication of America's intention to hit back against its enemy. Bombs dropped on Tokyo, Kobe, Yokohama and Nagoya did little damage and all the Mitchells crashed or force-landed. Most of the crews survived.

The Battle of the Coral Sea, in May 1942, was the first in history fought entirely by naval aircraft, with no gunfire between ships. It was indecisive. On the other hand, the Battle of Midway, in June 1942, changed the course of the Pacific War. Four Japanese carriers and a cruiser were sunk and the US Navy lost one carrier in each battle. Douglas TBD-1 Devastator torpedo bombers, like these on the USS *Enterprise*, suffered heavy casualties at Midway. One squadron was entirely destroyed and another decimated by Japanese Mitsubishi Zero fighters, and TBDs were withdrawn from operational use.

America's entry into the war brought its immense production capability to the Allied side. These assembly lines of Lockheed P-38 fighters had their counterparts in many states. Between January 1935 and September 1945, a total of 303,713 aeroplanes were manufactured in the USA.

In Europe, the strategic bombing offensive against Germany built to a climax. By day, the US Eighth Air Force, based in the UK, dispatched huge fleets of Boeing B-17 Fortresses and Convair B-24 Liberators. By night, RAF Bomber Command mounted raids of up to 1,000 aircraft, spearheaded by Avro Lancasters (pages 86-87) and Handley Page Halifaxes. The accuracy of the RAF attacks improved impressively as new radio and radar systems aided navigation and bomb-aiming. When North American P-51 Mustang fighters first escorted B-17s all the way to Berlin (above), Reichsmarschall Hermann Göring, Commander-in-Chief of the Luftwaffe, remarked gloomily: 'Germany has now lost the war'.

Equally depressing for Germany were the raids made by the RAF's de Havilland Mosquitos. Built of wood and unarmed, they were powered by the same Rolls-Royce Merlin engines as Hurricanes, Spitfires, Lancasters, Mustangs and other outstanding warplanes. Therefore, they were fast enough to elude enemy interceptors and, sometimes, made two attacks in a night. The 4,000lb bomb being loaded on this 415mph Mosquito B.Mk XVI of No.128 Squadron represented a heavier load than was carried by many four-engined Fortresses. Losses were one per 2,000 sorties by the time Mosquitos attacked Berlin from 30,000 to 40,000ft on thirty-six successive nights in February-March 1945.

Developed from a huge glider intended originally to support the invasion of Britain, the Messerschmitt Me 323 Gigant was a six-engined transport capable of carrying 130 troops on two decks, small tracked vehicles and supplies. Cruising speed was only 136mph and the defensive armament of five guns provided little protection on 22 April 1943 when twenty-one were shot down while attempting to ferry fuel to Rommel's Afrika Korps.

Used throughout the war as a personal transport for senior staff like Feldmarschalls Rommel and Kesselring in the field, and for army co-operation and ambulance duties, the Fieseler Storch set the pattern for generations of STOL (short take-off and landing) aircraft. A 240hp Argus engine, wing leading-edge slots and full-span flaps enabled it to take off in 213ft, land in 65ft and remain airborne at 32mph, carrying three people.

The success of German airborne forces in Western Europe in 1940 persuaded the UK government to form both paratroop and glider units. A total of 3,655 production Airspeed Horsa gliders, each capable of carrying twenty to twenty-five troops, were built for use everywhere from Norway, in 1942, to the Rhine crossing, in March 1945. Shown at Ta rrant Rushton airfield in Dorset are larger General Aircraft Hamilcars deployed for towing to the Rhine by Halifax tugs in a UK/US force of 1,326 gliders. Each could load a seven-ton tank or other freight through its hinged drive-in nose.

Rocket-firing Hawker Typhoons terrified German forces before and after D-Day by attacking rail targets, radar stations and tank divisions. Other Typhoons were the only fighter-bombers of their day able to carry 2,000lb of bombs. Together, they blasted a path for the Allied armies advancing into France.

The modern era of strategic cruise missiles began on 13 June 1944, when Hitler launched the first Fieseler Fi 103 pulsejet-powered flying bombs against London from France. Known to the Germans as Vergeltungswaffen 1 (reprisal weapon 1) and to the English as 'Doodlebugs', they were catapult or air-launched and cruised at about 400mph. Newly-introduced Hawker Tempests of Fighter Command had a maximum speed of 435mph, which enabled them to destroy 638 of the 1,771 V1s brought down by the RAF. In total, 2,419 hit London before the V1 was followed by the V2 rocket, against which the only defence was to destroy the launch sites.

One of a huge variety of German *wunderwaffen* (wonder weapons) conceived to stave off defeat, the 596mph Messerschmitt Me 163 Komet rocket-fighter was the first tail-less aircraft to enter service. With enough fuel for only eight minutes, endurance could be extended by switching off the rocket and gliding. About 300 were built, but their two 30mm guns tended to jam, they were tricky to land on a central skid, and pilots were killed or injured when the rocket fuels leaked or mixed and exploded in accidents. Me 163s were credited with only nine combat victories.

These Gloster Meteor F.Mk Is of No.616 Squadron were the first jet aircraft to enter RAF service. After shooting down thirteen V1s from their base at Manston, in Kent, they transferred to the Continent. There they were joined by other Meteors and were the only Allied jets used operationally in the Second World War. There were no jet-to-jet combats in 1944-1945, but a later Meteor F.4 showed its capability by raising the world speed record by nearly 30 per cent, to 606mph, in November 1945.

The Luftwaffe's Messerschmitt Me 262 jet fighter might have caused serious problems for the USAAF's daylight bomber offensive had it entered service earlier. Fully operational from 3 October 1944, units equipped with Me 262s achieved many successes against Allied piston-engined aircraft, but were overwhelmed numerically and suffered from fuel shortage and attacks on their airfields. As a result, more than 100 were lost. The maximum speed of the Me 262 was 536mph, compared with 415mph for the early Meteors.

Russian pilots had a reputation for ramming their opponents during both World Wars, but the tactic gained terrifying new significance when Japan mounted *Kamikaze* suicide missions against Allied naval vessels in the Pacific. In ten months, at enormous cost in volunteer pilots, *Kamikazes* accounted for 48% of all US warships damaged and 21% of those lost in the entire forty-four-month Pacific War. This Mitsubishi Zero, one of Japan's best fighters, is about to impact USS *Missouri*. Air-launched and piloted Ohka flying bombs were also used.

Boeing B-29 Superfortress bombers inflicted increasing devastation on the Japanese home islands, burning the heart out of sixty-six major cities. Unimaginable horror struck Hiroshima on 6 August 1945, when the first atomic bomb was dropped on the city from the B-29 *Enola Gay* (above). On 9 August a second atomic bomb fell on Nagasaki. On 15 August Japan surrendered and the Second World War ended. It was argued that the Allied/Japanese death toll would have been much higher had it been necessary to invade the home islands, but the effects of nuclear war were clearly so terrible that it became the 'big stick' of deterrence against a third world war for the remainder of the century.

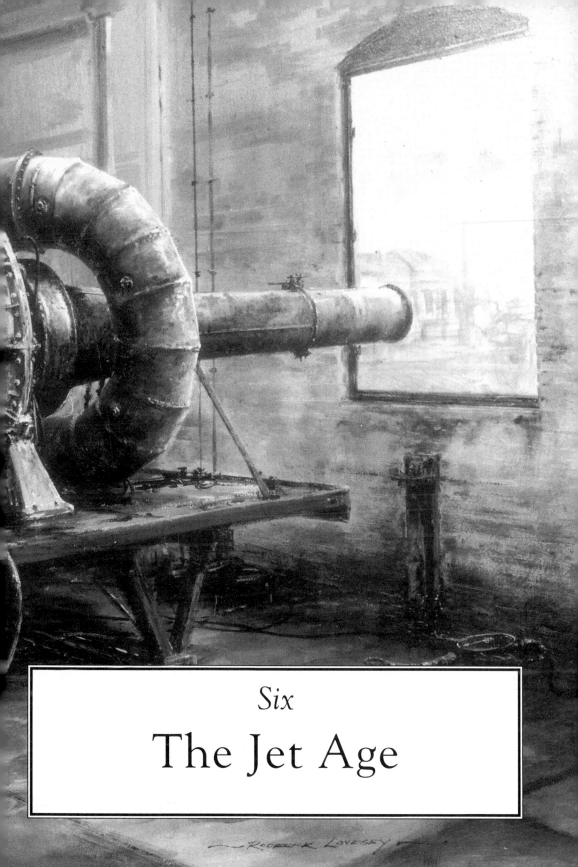

Six

The Jet Age

The first landing by a jet aircraft on an aircraft carrier was made by Lt Cdr E.M. Brown, RNVR, in this modified de Havilland Vampire on 3 December 1945. Fifteen landings and take-offs were made on HMS *Ocean* in two days.

The first piloted supersonic flight was made by Capt. Charles 'Chuck' Yeager, USAF, in the rocket-powered Bell X-1 research aircraft on 14 October 1947. The X-l, named *Glamorous Glennis* after his wife, was air-launched from a B-29 and accelerated to Mach 1.06 (700mph) at 45,000ft.

Previous page: Roderick Lovesey's painting shows Frank Whittle with his W/U experimental engine, which became the first turbojet in the world to be bench-tested, on 12 April 1937. The single wrap-round combustion chamber was replaced by ten small longitudinal chambers in 1938. A development of this design, the W.l, powered the Gloster E.28/39 which made the first flight by a British jet aircraft on 15 May 1941. Design of the Meteor jet fighter (page 104), with W.2B engines, had started in the previous year.

German wartime research showed that the dangerous effects of compressibility shock-waves, built up as aircraft approached the speed of sound, could be delayed by sweeping back the wings. The first post-war fighters to take advantage of this were the North American F-86 Sabre, flown on 1 October 1947, and the Soviet MiG-15, flown on 30 December 1947. The MiG had a British-supplied Rolls-Royce Nene turbojet and initiated a succession of high-quality MiG jet fighters that has continued to this day. This MiG-15bis served with the Czechoslovak Air Force. Armament comprised one 37mm and two 23mm guns.

Airfields had been built all over the globe during the Second World War, usually with concrete runways to accommodate military bombers and transports. Their availability post-war led to the rapid demise of large flying boats in airline service. Typical of their first-generation replacements was this Douglas DC-4 of KLM, used on freight services from Schiphol in the Netherlands. Larger DC-6s and DC-7s followed before piston-engines themselves gave way to jets.

When the Soviet Union closed all surface routes into the US, UK and French sectors of Berlin on 23 June 1948, the British responded by flying in supplies two days later. On the 26th, the Americans joined in what was to become the Berlin Airlift, followed by French and Commonwealth air forces and commercial operators. An average of 380 aircraft each day kept Berlin alive and at work even after the blockade was lifted on 12 May 1949 and the airlift ended on 30 September. RAF and British civilian aircraft, like these Avro Yorks, contributed 542,236 of the 2.3 million tons of cargo carried into the city. Together, the USAF and RAF flew a total of 104,358,951 miles, further than the distance from the earth to the sun, and prevented a third world war.

A unique air bridge to France was opened on 14 July 1948, when Silver City Airways flew a car and its four occupants by Bristol Freighter from Lympne Airport in Kent to Le Touquet, France. By 1955 it had built its own specialised terminal airport at Ferryfield; its fifteen aircraft carried 44,670 cars, 8,774 motor cycles and 166,219 passengers that year, each averaging 3,414 landings and take-offs. An aircraft took off every eighty-nine seconds; flight time on the shortest route, Ferryfield-Le Touquet, was twenty minutes. The fare for a small car was £5 and up to three could be carried by each Freighter.

The success of Igor Sikorsky's VS-300 prototype marked the start of the modern helicopter industry. First flown on 14 September 1939, its single-main-rotor design had been perfected by the spring of 1943, when control and stability were so precise that the designer was able to lift a small ring from a pole as part of his demonstrations.

The military helicopter proved its worth during the Korean War of 1950-1953. Casualty evacuation helicopters, like this US Navy Bell HTL-4, reduced to the lowest percentage in combat history the number of injured who died. Korea also brought the first victory by the pilot of one jet aircraft over another when Lt Russel J. Brown, USAF, flying a Lockheed F-80C Shooting Star, shot down a MiG-15 on 8 November 1950.

Convair's experimental XF-92A was the first powered delta-wing jet aircraft to fly, on 19 February 1949. Its purpose was to provide data for a Mach 1.5 fighter designed in consultation with Dr Alexander Lippisch, whose research and construction of deltas dated from 1926 and who had been responsible for the tail-less Me 163 rocket fighter. The XF-92A's basic configuration evolved into the USAF's supersonic Convair F-102A, and inspired generations of modern delta-wing aircraft.

Britain's early post-war lead in gas-turbine engines enabled it to pioneer jet-age airline travel. Vickers Viscount G-AHRF, powered by four Rolls-Royce Dart turboprops, operated the world's first scheduled passenger service by a gas-turbine powered airliner, in British European Airways colours, on 29 July 1950. A total of 445 were eventually sold, the final version carrying up to sixty-five passengers for 1,587 miles at 333mph.

The 490mph de Havilland Comet was the aircraft with which Britain hoped to gain world leadership in commercial transport design. During the Second World War, it had concentrated on producing military aircraft, while the US developed what became the first generation of great post-war piston-engined transports. BOAC began the first scheduled passenger service with turbojet airliners from London to Johannesburg, South Africa, with G-ALYP, one of its ten thirty-six-seat Comet 1s, on 2 May 1952. Subsequent accidents, found to be caused by the hitherto-unsuspected problem of fatigue in a highly-pressurised cabin, led to grounding of the Comets. By the time the aircraft had been redesigned as the Comet 4, the US had regained leadership with the larger, longer-range Boeing 707. However, Comet 4s operated the world's first transatlantic jet passenger services from 4 October 1958.

Rollout of the prototype for the USAF's KC-135 flight refuelling tanker and the Boeing 707 airliner at Renton, Washington, on 14 May 1954. It flew for the first time on 15 July. Pan American began transatlantic passenger services with production 707-121s, seating between 124 and 179 passengers, on 26 October 1958. Their cruising speed of 571mph revolutionised long-distance air travel. Eventually, 1,010 Model 707s and similar 720s were completed for worldwide use, including a few for specialized military purposes.

Lockheed's U-2 was developed in the company's highly-secret Skunk Works as essentially a lightweight jet-powered aircraft for covert reconnaissance missions over the Soviet Union. The loss of one, shot down near Sverdlovsk on 1 May 1960, caused international tension, but operations over many parts of the world continued even after satellites began to provide round-the-clock surveillance. The U-2R illustrated had a maximum speed of 430mph and range of more than 3,000 miles at above 70,000ft.

Designed as commercial transports, the first Lockheed Constellations were taken over by the USAAF in the Second World War; many others were bought subsequently, in parallel with post-war airliner versions. Of special importance were airborne early warning variants like this EC-121H Super Constellation of USAF Air Defense Command. Target-tracking and special communications equipment enabled it to extend greatly the coverage of surface-based radars, with instantaneous relay of data to ground stations. The task is handled today by such aircraft as the Boeing E-3 Sentry, with over-fuselage rotating radar 'saucer'.

Leland Snow crop-dusting cabbages in Texas with his S-2 prototype in 1956. At the age of twenty-three he had decided that the conversions of old civil and military aircraft used for agricultural work since war-surplus Curtiss Jennies had begun dusting Louisiana cotton fields in 1922 were inadequate and dangerous. His S-1 and S-2 seated the pilot high, to minimise danger in a crash landing, setting the pattern for many new purpose-built agricultural aircraft. The products of his Air Tractor company outlived competition from Cessna, Piper and others. Its largest current turboprop-powered model, with a useful load of more than four tons, is also used worldwide for firefighting and eradicating oil slicks.

Small jet aircraft for personal and VIP transportation date from 7 October 1963, when Bill Lear's first Learjet 23 flew at Wichita, Kansas. It was designed to carry up to seven passengers at more than 500mph and was equipped with a refreshment cabinet, table and toilet. The larger and more luxurious executive jets of today, including 1990s Learjets, sometimes carry nineteen passengers and offer transatlantic range.

Private flying had increased rapidly after the Second World War. In Australia few large sheep and cattle stations were without a landing strip by the mid-1960s, enabling aircraft like this Cessna to link them with distant towns. The Cessna company expected to produce 10,000 aircraft a year until a sudden huge increase in fuel prices in the 1970s, allied to a spate of absurd litigation claims, almost put the US lightplane industry out of business for years.

The Cold War that had existed between NATO and nations of the Warsaw Pact since the Berlin Airlift underwrote huge military aircraft production. In 1964, USAF's General Dynamics F-111 introduced variable-geometry wings that could be set at 16° sweepback for take-off and swung back to 72.5° for flight at up to Mach 2.5. Terrain-following radar enabled high-speed attack at very low level, under the search field of enemy surface radar. After a disappointing start, F-111 fighter-bombers gave good service in the Vietnam War of 1961-1975.

Armed helicopters entered widespread use in Vietnam, to escort troop-carrying and ambulance helicopters and to suppress enemy ground forces. The first were standard utility Bell HU-1Bs like this, with guns or rocket pods mounted on each side of the cabin. Bell then adapted the design into the slender-fuselage two-seat AH-1 HueyCobra, offering less of a target for ground fire and with heavier armament. This set a standard for modern combat helicopters, which can carry anti-tank missiles and a wide range of avionics and equipment for target seeking and precision attack in all weathers.

Designed as the primary air component of America's airborne, submarine and silo-based nuclear deterrent force, the eight-jet Boeing B-52 Stratofortress was used as a conventional bomber in Vietnam. The eighty-five late-model B-52Hs in current service can each carry twelve air-launched cruise missiles, which they have used, with conventional warheads, against targets in Iraq and Serbia. TV and infra-red sensors and GPS ensure navigational accuracy, electronic countermeasures and the ability to launch missiles from long stand-off range enhance defence and the ALCMs provide pinpoint accuracy of attack.

The fastest military aircraft to enter service in the twentieth century, Lockheed's SR-71 Blackbird was an unarmed two-seat strategic reconnaissance aircraft that supplemented U-2s from 1966 for more than three decades without fear of interception. Construction was largely of titanium, to withstand sustained high temperatures in flight. The end-of-century absolute aeroplane speed record of 2,193mph and sustained horizontal height record of 85,069ft, set under official rules, were set by an SR-71 on 28 July 1976.

Air-launched from a B-52, the rocket-powered North American X-15A-2 research aircraft was the fastest aeroplane ever flown. Piloted by W.J. Knight, it attained 4,534mph (Mach 6.72) on 3 October 1967. The greatest height reached by one of the three X-15s was 354,200ft, by J.A. Walker on 22 August 1963. At extreme altitudes its pilots qualified for US astronaut's wings.

Humanitarian work continues to be a primary task for aircraft throughout the Third World. This STOL de Havilland Turbo-Beaver, belonging to the British Mission Aviation Fellowship fleet, is shown arriving at Tulegit in a remote part of Ethiopia. Access to these Surma people from Addis Ababa takes two or more days overland, including use of dugout canoes for part of the year. The Beaver takes two hours to bring in essential supplies, mission team members and visitors, and to act as an air ambulance to carry the Surma to hospital when necessary.

Lockheed Hercules transports, designed originally for military use, have long been the heroes of airborne relief for regions plagued by natural and man-made disasters. These Rwandan children gathered to wait for food delivered by an L-100-30 Hercules of Southern Air Transport under Project Support Hope, which airlifted thousands of tons of supplies into refugee camps in Zaire after the Rwandan massacres of the mid-1990s.

First flown on 23 October 1967, the Canadair CL-215 is a purpose-designed replacement for the hundreds of converted civil and military aircraft used to drop water and fire retardant on burning forests and other sites. Its amphibian design enables it to operate from unprepared small airstrips or lakes. It scoops up water while flying low over lakes or rivers at around 70mph and can drop more than 120,000 gallons in over 100 flights in a single day. Current improved CL-415s are turboprop-powered.

The Martin Marietta X-24A, Northrop/NASA M2-F3 and Northrop/NASA HL-10 were wingless lifting-body research aircraft flight tested between 1966 and 1971 to study the feasibility of manoeuvring and landing an aerodynamic craft designed for re-entry from space. Air-launched by a B-52 mother-ship, they flew under rocket power before making unpowered landings that contributed to development of the Space Shuttle.

The go-anywhere capability of helicopters has enabled them to find ever-increasing use, none more important than carrying personnel and supplies to offshore oil and gas rigs. This nineteen to twenty-four-passenger Eurocopter Super Puma is one of the large fleet that services North Sea rigs. Worldwide, helicopters also perform flying crane, rescue, paramedic and ambulance missions that would be impossible for any other vehicle.

New possibilities for low-fare mass travel to the farthest parts of the world were opened up by the Boeing 747 when it first flew on 9 February 1969. The 1990s Model 747-400, shown in British Airways markings, can carry up to 524 passengers, with seventy-six on a short upper deck.

24 May 1976. Supersonic air travel came to the USA when Concordes of British Airways and Air France flew the first Mach 2 services to Dulles, Washington, over the Atlantic from Europe. At premium fares, these unique Anglo-French airliners have offered completely safe and luxurious transportation for up to 100 passengers for almost a quarter of a century, although the 'sonic boom' produced during supersonic flight has restricted them largely to overwater routes.

The largest aeroplane yet put into production and service is the An-124 freighter built by Antonov of Kiev in Ukraine, with a span of 240ft 5¾in and maximum loaded weight of 864,200lb in its commercial form. With a payload of up to 118 tons, this An-124 operated by Air Foyle of the UK easily accommodated a 35-ton cryogenic pressure vessel and its smaller 25-ton companion in one flight from Paris to Budapest. In May 1987 an An-124 set a distance record by flying 12,521 miles non-stop in 25½ hours.

One of the trials of the jet age is that it often takes longer to travel from the centre of a city like London to its primary terminal airport than the flight time from there to Paris. A remedy was offered when quiet turbofan-powered airliners like these BAe 146/Avro RJs followed earlier turboprop types into London City Airport, built in former docklands only six miles from the Bank of England.

Since the 1970s, the Airbus Industrie consortium, with airframe prime contractors in France, Germany, the UK and Spain, has provided steadily increased competition for Boeing. From the start, its products benefited from highly-advanced wing design. Airbus A320s, shown under construction in 1990, were the first subsonic commercial transports to have composites primary structures, computerised fly-by-wire control instead of a mechanical system, side-stick controllers instead of the usual control column and aileron wheel, and an automatic flight control system guaranteeing entirely new standards of efficiency.

The difficulties encountered by the US lightplane industry led to a rapid growth in the numbers of aircraft built by amateurs from kits and plans. The total registered by the Federal Aviation Administration increased from 2,865 in 1971 to 19,409 in 1997. The Experimental Aircraft Association's annual AirVenture Oshkosh meeting in Wisconsin in 1998 attracted 682 of them in the world's biggest air show gathering of 800,000 people and 12,000 aircraft over seven days.

Tilt-rotor aircraft of the kind pioneered by the Bell Boeing V-22 Osprey combine the vertical/short take-off (V/STOL) capability of a helicopter with the performance of a fixed-wing turboprop. For take-off the 6,150shp wingtip turboshafts pivot so that the three-blade prop-rotors act in helicopter mode. Airborne, they tilt forward, enabling the prop-rotors to function as propellers. In its transport form the V-22 carries twenty-four combat-equipped troops, cargo or twelve stretchers over a 230 mile radius at 288mph. Smaller civil tilt-rotors are under development.

To survive in modern combat, aircraft embody 'stealth' techniques to reduce their signature (image) on enemy radars. First to maximise stealth was the USAF's F-117A Nighthawk, built at Lockheed Martin's Skunk Works. The airframe skin panels are divided into many small perfectly flat surfaces that reflect hostile radar signals in a variety of directions. Much of the surface is made of radar-absorbent composites. The intakes and exhausts of the low-noise engines are above the wings to shield them from infra-red seekers below. Primary armament comprises internally-stowed 2,000lb bombs with laser guidance for pinpoint accuracy.

Voted best of the military aerobatic display teams that fly the flag for air forces internationally is the Royal Air Force's Red Arrows. Its nine British Aerospace Hawk trainers were photographed passing the statue of Mother Russia, overlooking the River Dnieper, near Kiev, in July 1990, during the first visit by a western air force unit to the Soviet Union for almost fifty years.

The Harrier was the first modern combat aircraft able to dispense with the need for vulnerable runways by its V/STOL capability. By vectoring the four exhaust nozzles of its Pegasus turbofan downward, it can thrust itself vertically into the air. Partial deflection permits short take-off with a heavier weapon load. The RAF Harrier II GR.7 illustrated is a second-generation version. It is built jointly by McDonnell Douglas (Boeing) and BAe, with a one-piece carbon-fibre wing, doubled payload or range, and much-enhanced offensive and defensive systems. Harrier IIs serve also with the US Marine Corps and Italian and Spanish Navies.

For more than a decade, Swedish Air Force fighter squadrons have trained for wartime dispersal by operating from stretches of roadway and conducting refuelling, re-arming and other between-flights servicing in the shelter of roadside trees. The aircraft shown is one of its latest Saab JAS 39 Gripens, the world's first fourth-generation jet combat aircraft, which can be reconfigured quickly for alternative interceptor, attack or reconnaissance duties. Like many 1990s deltas, it has foreplanes for enhanced handling.

More than sixty years of work on flying-wing aircraft culminated in Northrop's choice of this wholly unconventional configuration for the USAF's B-2 Spirit 'stealth' bomber. First flown on 17 July 1989, this four-jet subsonic aircraft spans 172ft, has a range of more than 11,500 miles with one flight refuelling, and can carry nearly eighteen tons of nuclear or conventional weapons. Only twenty-one have been built, each costing $2.1 billion.

Flying entered a new dimension on 12 April 1961, when Soviet cosmonaut Yury Gagarin made the first orbit of the Earth from space in the spherical, rocket-launched Vostok capsule. Eight years later, on 20 July 1969, as US astronaut Neil Armstrong stepped down onto the surface of the moon from his Eagle spacecraft, he remarked 'That's one small step for a man, one giant leap for mankind.' As the twentieth century ends, NASA Space Shuttle missions, of the kind shown being launched, are commonplace. Although shaped as an aeroplane, the spacecraft is best regarded as a manoeuvrable rocket for tasks in orbit at a speed of approximately 17,600mph. It lands as a glider, using aerodynamic controls, at a touchdown speed of 212-226mph.

Epilogue

With the advent of a new millennium, much of the challenge and adventure of aviation has faded along with the twentieth century. The 1.5 billion passengers who travel each year on scheduled airline services seldom see much from aircraft that fly most of the time under automatic pre-programmed control. In the military field, even the USA is unlikely to afford a further generation of manned strategic bombers after the B-2. Unmanned air vehicles are taking over reconnaissance duties, supplementing orbital satellites. In the future, it may be that only those who fly lightplanes, microlights, gliders and balloons will enjoy *real* flying of the kind that aviation's pioneers and later men and women of courage made possible in our century of flight.